BEYOND POSSIBLE

The Simple Formula for Living the Life You Desire

JENNIFER EMMETT

First published by Ultimate World Publishing 2020
Copyright © 2020 Jennifer Emmett

ISBN

Paperback - 978-1-922372-48-2
Ebook - 978-1-922372-49-9

Jennifer Emmett has asserted her right under the Copyright, Designs and Patents Act 1988 to be identified as the author of this work. The information in this book is based on the author's experiences and opinions. The publisher specifically disclaims responsibility for any adverse consequences, which may result from use of the information contained herein. Permission to use information has been sought by the author. Any breaches will be rectified in further editions of the book.

All rights reserved. No part of this publication may be reproduced, stored in or introduced into a retrieval system, or transmitted in any form, or by any means (electronic, mechanical, photocopying, recording or otherwise) without the prior written permission of the author. Any person who does any unauthorised act in relation to this publication may be liable to criminal prosecution and civil claims for damages. Enquiries should be made through the publisher.

Cover design: Ultimate World Publishing
Layout and typesetting: Ultimate World Publishing
Cover photo: Tala-Natali/shutterstock.com
Editor: Hayley Ward

Ultimate World Publishing
Diamond Creek,
Victoria Australia 3089
www.writeabook.com.au

Testimonials

"I have known and worked with Jennifer Emmett over the past ten years. Jennifer is one of the great role models and inspiring leaders in our community. Jennifer always thrives on empowering the people around her to aim high and reach out to be the very best they can.

Jennifer's participative leadership style enables her and her team to achieve not only the organisation goals but also their personal goals. Jennifer's leadership skill set is very valuable to delivering on the company goals.

Jennifer's welcoming, friendly and positive approach to life is infectious to whoever meets her. This positive outlook enables Jennifer to achieve her personal goals and cut through trying and difficult times when there didn't seem to be any way forward. Jennifer always rises above the difficulties to emerge on the other side in a bigger and better way.

Congratulations, Jennifer, on achieving another one of your life's goals. I can't wait to read your book. I know it will be a bestseller."

Cr Karen May, Deputy Mayor, *Mackay Regional Council*

"Jennifer's book is very well done. The minute I started reading it, I knew it was exactly what I was looking for to complement her business coaching sessions. I have read many books about self-development, how to change habits and leadership – but I always had trouble putting the theories into action. This is different as it combines all the best theory with Jennifer's real life experience of creating her good life. I have seen Jennifer change from a shy and insecure child to a confident, loving and caring leader in her field. She has overcome many obstacles and challenges in her life by embracing and accepting they are all part of who she is.

This book is clear, concise and practical. Jennifer's openness and honesty in her personal stories is inspiring. It covers so much more than I expected. The Good Life Game plan is an added bonus that I look forward to using."
   Karen Young, *Chief Organiser, iTidy Organising*

"Jen's book, Beyond Possible, provides achievable tools that anyone will be able to use in their everyday thoughts and lifestyle choices. The consistent theme of being able to 'reprogram' your autopilot, is one I could really connect with, along with the ABCDE concept of which we can train ourselves to look at negative behaviours in a different way.

The personal anecdotes that Jen has included are what make this book both powerful and relatable. A lot of motivational books can be overwhelming with the hundreds of pages of ideas and techniques, however Jen's book is concise and down to earth, which is what makes it so easy to identify

TESTIMONIALS

with. I could certainly relate to the concepts and notions provided in the book and I look forward to putting these tools into practice."

Toni Hamilton, *Finance Manager*

"Several years ago, I realised I was living my life on autopilot. I had a loving husband, two happy, healthy kids, lived in a great area, had a lovely comfortable home and a good job, but the kids were growing up and starting to lead lives of their own. I had not dared to dream or make any plans for what our good life could be beyond giving our kids a loving home and every opportunity to succeed. I then spent 12 months working through all aspects of my preferred reality with Jennifer. The support, encouragement and kind understanding that Jennifer provided was life-changing, and I am thankful that I have been enjoying My Good Life. Jennifer's book Beyond Possible is great to have on hand with the inspirational stories and easy to understand and use tools to check back in with myself to ensure I continue enjoying My Good Life."

Linda Farrell, *Chief Finance Officer*

"From the beginning right to the end, Beyond Possible has me believing that 'my good life' is very much within my reach. Jennifer is inspirational as she vulnerably grounds her writing in personal experience while sharing a wealth of well-tested tools and processes that have enabled her to achieve her dreams. Hers is a lived reality which I have had the enormous pleasure of experiencing as a drumming teacher, supporting both myself and my students, then later as a personal and business coach. Jennifer's energy and creativity combined with her reflectiveness shines as she interacts with others and, in Beyond Possible, she offers this to us all."

Sue Vonthien

Dedication

Laurel
You have always been the perfect Mum for me.
I cherish every moment with you.

Contents

Testimonials	iii
Dedication	vii
Introduction	1
Part 1: Let the Treasure Hunt Begin	9
Part 2: Finding the Map	27
Part 3: Adventure Bound	43
Part 4 : Surprising Discoveries	65
Part 5: Finding Affinity	87
Part 6: To Infinity and Beyond	95
Part 7: Forecasting the Future	113
Part 8: The Adventure Seeker Essentials	123
Part 9: Lights... Camera... Action	135
Part 10: Cue the Music	153
Afterword	167
Appendices	171
About the Author	179
More Testimonials	181

Introduction

There is a technique called the Johari window that helps people to better understand their relationship with themselves and others. It's designed to help us understand what is known about ourselves, and it breaks this knowing into four quadrants.

> One - Known to self and known to others.
> Two - Known to self but not known to others.
> Three - Not known to self but known to others.
> Four - Not known to self and not known to others[1].

Former US politician Donald Rumsfeld made this concept famous in his 2002 report where he said "there are known knowns; there are things we know we know. We also know there are known unknowns; that is to say, we know there are some things we do not know. But there are also unknown unknowns—the ones we don't know we don't know"[2].

Johari Window

Joseph Luft (1916-2014) & Harrington Ingham (1916 - 1995)

	Known to Self	Not Known to Self
Known to Others	Things about you that both you and others know. **Arena or Open Self**	Things about you that you don't know but others do know. **Blind Spot or Unaware Self**
Not Known to Others	Things about you that you know but others don't know. **Facade or Hidden Self**	Things about you that you don't know and others don't know. **Unknown**

In writing this book, I started to gain a better understanding of the things I know, the things I used to know but forgot and the things I want to know. I also came to understand and accept that some knowings will come to me in time and some knowings will never come to me.

I believe the pursuit of knowledge can bring a great sense of purpose, and I understand that there are many different ways for us to engage in learning about our inner and outer lives.

Throughout history, humans have shared stories, theatre, books, music, art, poetry, and we each form our own knowings from this sharing.

I left school when I was 16 years old because I could not see how further education had anything to do with me. I did not know what I wanted to do or be. I thought that I was not very smart, so my options were limited. By the time I was 18, I had been working as a shop assistant for two years. I knew that I was uneducated, and I was discovering things about myself that led me to believe that I would spend the rest of my life alone. At the same time, I made a

INTRODUCTION

decision that I wanted to have a good life. I consider that decision to be the single most important decision of my life. In making the decision to have a good life, I started to imagine what my good life would be. I started to consider the possibilities and I turned those possibilities into my reality. In fact, my life now is well beyond what that 18-year-old thought was possible.

What life do you imagine for yourself?

In this book, I am sharing with you how I turned my imagined life into my actual life. I am sharing some of my experiences and current knowings. I leave it entirely up to you to decide if this knowledge is useful for you or not.

Our Imagination Tool

I like the analogy that our brain is like a computer and our unconscious mind is the computer program or autopilot. When you think about it, the computer was invented to do what the human mind could already do. Originally the word "computer" referred to a person who spent their days adding and subtracting numbers and entering the results into tables so that other people could use these tables to complete tasks. A guy by the name of Charles Babbage spent years designing a table-making machine in an effort to reproduce and speed up what human computers could do. He developed the plans for the Analytical Engine which resemble the component of today's computers. It had a central processing unit (CPU) and a memory; he called them the mill and the store. He also had a device called the "reader" to input instructions and then an output device called the printer[3].

Like a computer, our mind can receive information. It can process this information based on a set of programmed protocols, and it can output responses to this information.

Of course, the human brain and a computer are different, and one of these differences is that the human mind has the capacity to imagine. If our brain is alive then our imagination is alive and we can consciously and unconsciously use our imagination to dream, create art, music, theatre, architecture, gardens, food and games. We can use our imagination to develop new inventions and concepts and we can consciously use our imagination to create the life we want for ourselves.

Acknowledging that the human brain and mind are different to a computer, there are some useful comparisons, so I use the brain/computer analogy to help explain how we can use our mind to change our life.

Sometimes computer programs can be frustrating; they just won't do what you want them to do. Have you ever felt that frustration? You tried and tried over and over to input the information and get what you needed but it just did not work, no matter what you did. Eventually, in desperation, you raised a support request and a programmer tweaked the program and now it works just the way you want it to work.

You can learn to be the programmer who tweaks your own program so that it creates the life you want for yourself. There are lots of tools you can use, and I will discuss many in this book. I also encourage you to explore and find the ones that are right for you.

I think a lot about thinking and how we can use our thoughts to create the life we want. I also believe that it is important to balance

INTRODUCTION

this thinking activity by allowing the time and space to not think. Allowing ourselves to just be and knowing that that is enough.

As I wrote this book, I realised that over the years I have developed and/or used a whole set of practical tools to assist me in creating my good life and that these tools may be useful to you. I have made some of these practical tools available for you to download for free from my website www.thevillageleaders.com.au. I have also included the instructions for many of the activities in the appendices of this book. I encourage you to use an A4 exercise book as you make your plan and keep it well organised because you will need to find your information as you read through this book and create your Good Life Game Plan.

You can also access some free online tools to help you incorporate these activities into your daily life, including the **Wheel of Life, ABCDE of My Feelings and Actions** and the **My Life Planning App**.

For those of you who do not want to make your own plan, I have created the **Good Life Game Plan Pack**. This pack includes the **Good Life Game Plan** companion manual with the full set of practical tools to assist you to do all of the activities I discuss in this book, plus the **My Good Life online course**. It systematically guides you through the whole process, and you can easily see your progress along the way.

You can purchase the **Good Life Game Plan Pack** from www.thevillageleaders.com.au.

I love to hear what people are doing to create the life they desire. You can sign up for free to the **Beyond Possible Facebook** group and share your stories as you progress through this book. It could just be that your story inspires someone else to have a better life.

BEYOND POSSIBLE

You can also follow me on Facebook or contact me through my website www.thevillageleaders.com.au.

You have powers you
never dreamed of.

You can do things you
never thought you could do.

There are no limitations
in what you can do
except for the limitations
in your own mind as to
what you cannot do.

Don't think you cannot.

Think you can.

Darwin P. Kingsley

PART 1
Let the Treasure Hunt Begin

Good[4]

Adjective
1. To be desired or approved of
2. Having the required qualities; of a high standard
3. Possessing or displaying moral virtue
4. Giving pleasure; enjoying or satisfying
5. Thorough
6. Valid

Noun
1. That which is morally right; righteous
2. Benefit or advantage to someone or something

Adverb
1. Well

Take a minute to ask yourself these questions.
- What would make my life good?
- What would I be like?
- What would I do?
- What would I have?

Do you have clearly defined answers to these questions? Don't worry if you don't because most people don't. I often hear people say things like:
- I know I am smart enough to do lots of things and I could be successful in my career, but I just don't know what I want to do.
- I really love this person, but I am unhappy in this relationship.
- My life is really boring.
- I never have enough time to do what I want to do.
- I never have enough money.
- I feel really distressed/anxious.
- I feel lonely and lost.
- I feel like I am supposed to do something in life, but I don't know what it is.

If you have ever said or thought any of these types of things, you are definitely not alone.

LET THE TREASURE HUNT BEGIN

These are quite common thoughts and feelings. Many people struggle to know what they want in life or what they can do about making it happen.

The thing is, we can't get what we want if we don't know what we want, and we can't know what we want if we don't make the space to think about it.

People often invest a lot of their valuable time and effort into thinking about what they don't want, and they end up feeling unsatisfied and unhappy in life.

It's common for us to hold false beliefs like:
- If I just had more money all of my problems would be solved.
- If I owned that nice new flash car/boat/gadget I would feel happier.
- If I was just skinnier/better looking/had lots of nice clothes all would be right with my world.

It is easy to understand why we form these types of false beliefs. We are constantly bombarded with messages produced by people who aim to exploit our very human nature to sell their products and services to us.

While we do need to have enough money to pay for our housing, food, health, transportation, education, sport, social activities, holidays, etc. and there is absolutely nothing wrong with earning enough money to afford luxury items and experiences, the material gain in itself will not lead us down the road of personal fulfilment. If we only focus on material gain and our external image, we can end up on the road to regret and dissatisfaction with life.

If we only invest our time and energy into one or two aspects of our lives, we will be limiting ourselves and missing out on many things that make life great.

Do you know how to find your balance in relation to family, friends, relationships, career, finances, health, personal development, spirituality, etc.?

Have you made a decision to live your good life?

In this chapter, you will learn why you need to know what makes life good for you.

You will start to understand the difference between material gain and personal fulfilment, and you will have the opportunity to learn more about your dreams.

Luck or Good Planning?

A number of years ago, I came to the conclusion that I was one of the luckiest people I knew. It's not that I thought that there was anything particularly special about me, it was just that I was living a life that the younger version of me could only dream about. I had fulfilled that young woman's dreams, I had more dreams and fulfilled them, and I could look back through my life and see a pattern of going beyond possible.

Let me tell you a little about that very young woman. I am going to talk about her in the third person because while I was her, she is not who I am now. In fact, there have been many versions of me since then, and I am grateful for these other versions and regularly thank them for the experience and knowledge they brought to my current life.

This young woman had no idea that she would morph from school drop-out to company CEO, be recognised by her local community for her down to earth leadership skills, fall in love, break hearts, be heartbroken, buy her first home, run a magazine, run a recycling centre, get paid to help other people, buy an investment property, make friends, lose friends, make more friends, buy a bigger home, become a musician, have regular holidays, be healthy, learn to meditate, become the leader of a drumming band, perform at all sorts of events, sing, get married, share many joyous meals and events with family and friends, have the luxury of time to pursue her passions, live in a loving home, feel a sense of achievement, and have enough money to live a comfortable life….and the adventure continues.

When she was six years old, someone decided, for reasons not known to her, it was a good idea to take this young girl out of her family for six weeks, put her on a train, with strangers, and send her over 700kms away to live in dorm accommodation with lots of other kids. This experience resulted in her putting her head down and trying not to be noticed; she did not want to be sent back there again. At 16 she dropped out of school because the education system had taught her that she was not very smart; she knew further education was not an option for her. She did not know what she wanted to do, she just knew that school was not for her. Luckily, her big sister got her a job in a delicatessen and she went to work each day because she knew she needed to earn money to pay her own way in life.

After about six months, the manager of the delicatessen left, and before she left, she gave the 16-year-old a parting gift. I can't remember the gift, but I will never forget the words on the front of the card. It read:

You have powers you never dreamed of. You can do things you never thought you could do. There are no limitations in what you can do except for the limitations in your own mind as to what you cannot do. Don't think you cannot. Think you can.

Darwin P. Kingsley

Back then, there was no social media and we did not see wise quotes daily. She was not a reader, so this was the first time in her life she had read words like that. Words that said she had powers, words that said she could do things and that she just needed to think "I can". She held that card often and read those words over and over. She thought about their meaning and she believed.

The spark of possibility was ignited and while in phases of my life it has been dimmed, it has never gone out; it is always there waiting for the next opportunity to make my good life.

Discovering a System of Success

She spent her childhood living in regional Queensland towns, and when she was 17, she moved to Brisbane and secured a job in a different delicatessen. Although her bosses were good to her, there were a couple of slightly older girls who bullied the 17-year-old, so she put her head down and worked harder.

When she went to that franchise's first Christmas party, she saw something she had not known happened in workplaces. The franchise annually recognised their State's best shop assistant. She watched in amazement when a young woman's name was called out and the whole room applauded her achievement. This young woman was presented with a sash and a prize, but the most important thing was the recognition of her hard work.

The 17-year-old felt that spark of possibility warm her from the inside and over the coming days, she set her goal of having her name announced at the annual Christmas awards night. She knew that she was not the smartest person, but she was a reliable worker and she was already pretty good at her job. She could also see what it took to be a good shop assistant. Over the next 12 months, she went to work every day with that vision in her mind of being called up and recognised for her work. She was quick to serve customers, she was welcoming and attentive, she created rapport with the regular customers, she did suggestive selling, she kept the stock levels high, she regularly stepped outside to look at the displays from the customer's point of view and made changes where it was needed, she listened to the bosses and did what they asked her to do, and when the bullies tried to set her up, she just let her hard work and integrity show the bosses that she was a good and reliable worker.

She went to the next annual Christmas awards night with so much hope in her heart. When it came time for the awards ceremony her name was not called, and she was disappointed. The next day she asked herself what else she could do to be the one person who stood out across the whole State. She spent the next 12 months with that vision in her mind. She stuck to the plan and increased her efforts to be the best shop assistant she could possibly be. She also quietly set her vision on, one day, being a shop manager. She observed the bosses and willingly engaged in any opportunity to learn new skills. That year at the annual Christmas awards, her name was called, and she understood what it felt like to achieve a goal she had set for herself.

That younger version of me had unwittingly stumbled across a system that would benefit me for my entire life. A system that has helped fulfil so many of my dreams and create the life I want for myself.

One: She imagined the possibilities, and she dreamed about it
- To be the best shop assistant in the State for that franchise.

Two: She turned her dream into a measurable goal
- To win Shop Assistant of the Year at the next Christmas party.

Three: She established her action plan
- Wherever possible, be the first to serve the customers.
- Be welcoming and attentive.
- Create rapport with the regulars.
- Increase shop revenue with suggestive selling.
- Keep the stock levels high and well presented.
- Observe and listen to the bosses.
- Actively engage in learning new skills.

Four: She worked on her mindset
- In her own mind, she regularly saw herself at the Christmas party walking up to the stage to collect the Shop Assistant of the Year sash.

Five: She committed to her goal and displayed resilience
- Even when it was hard, she turned up to work every day and did the best job she could.
- She did not let the bullies distract her from her plan.

- When she did not win the award at the first Christmas party, she stuck to the plan and increased her efforts to achieve her goal.

She was so amazed by this outcome that she decided to see if she could do it again …two years later she was again awarded Shop Assistant of the Year.

Achieving these goals confirmed in her own mind that the words on that card were true; she had powers, she just needed to think and focus on "I can" rather than getting trapped into thinking "I cannot". This gave her the courage to imagine more possibilities and more dreams, set more goals to go beyond what was currently possible in her life.

- She had changed her mindset, which changed her life.
- She had become more confident in her own abilities.
- The bosses had noticed her commitment to her work.
- They offered her a promotion, which she accepted.
- She was now in charge of the older girls who had bullied her, and they moved on.
- She now had a job that she absolutely loved. She was given opportunities to learn about leadership and continue to work on her personal development.

She now knew that if she made the commitment to invest in herself, if she did the actions and kept doing them even when things got tough, other people would step in and assist her to achieve her dreams.

HYHM Theory

I later developed this knowing into my HYHM theory.

Think about this....there are people all around you who know that one of the secrets of living a good and fulfilling life is to do things that help others, do things just because you can and ask for nothing in return.

So.....there are people walking around your world right now looking for the right opportunities to help others.

When you do things to help yourself, display a commitment to your goals through your thoughts, words and actions and keep your mind and heart open, all sorts of opportunities will present themselves to you, people will help you in ways that you could have never dreamed of.

I call this my HYHM (Help You Help Me) theory.

It was this HYHM theory that supported me to achieve my goal of being awarded the best shop assistant in Queensland for that franchise. I made the commitment, I said positive words to my customers and my bosses, I did the actions. My bosses nominated me for the award, they backed me, and they continued to back me by offering me a promotion, they exposed me to numerous learning and self-development opportunities, they invested in me because I had invested in myself.

Here is another example of how I imagined a new possibility, turned it into a goal, made a commitment to my goal, made a plan and started doing the actions.

First, I will set the scene. As a very young adult, I had formed the belief that I would be on my own for my entire life. I believed this because I knew that I was attracted to women, not men. My Catholic upbringing had taught me that only sinners would act on such impulses, so I had persisted with trying to have a normal life by dating men. I only ever had two serious boyfriends, and both were very good to me. I knew I had hurt my last boyfriend because he had wanted to get married and I just did not feel that way. I promised myself that I would never have another boyfriend because I did not want to enter another relationship knowing that I would never be able to return the love and commitment if it was offered to me.

I spent years crying myself to sleep and believing I was most likely the only woman like this in Australia. You may laugh and think that is a ridiculously naïve belief, and it was, but it was my truth at the time because I had not seen any alternative option in my life. Little did I know that once I opened that door there were women like me everywhere. By the time I reached my mid 20's, I had been through a list of short-term lovers and had sabotaged the loving relationships that were offered to me. I felt distress and grief at the loss of these relationships and had tried to suppress these feelings with cigarettes, alcohol, other drugs and by moving onto the next short-term relationship.

My own thoughts, words and actions had taken me off track, and I was not living my good life. I was living in crisis mode. I did not have enough money to pay for my housing, food, health, transportation, clothing etc. so along with the feelings of grief and loss, I had the constant knock of financial stress on my door.

Through this time, I experienced unemployment, housing insecurity, breakups and breakdown.

Along with the financial stress, a new acquaintance came knocking at my door and it did not wait to be invited in. It seeped through the gaps around the door, it came in through the windows and up through the floorboards. Before I knew it, depression had moved in, wrapped its arms around me and sucked the energy out of me. Feelings of overwhelming sadness and hopelessness enveloped me, I withdrew from my friends, my flatmate asked me to move out and I found myself living amongst strangers in a life where I did not belong. Fortunately, these strangers shared their music with me and for the first time in my life I picked up a guitar and I started to sing.

The depression was surprised by this newfound joy in my heart, so it let go and took a step back. It did not go away, it just waited for the effects of the music to stop so that it could slip back into its comfortable hold on me.

I kept learning the guitar and singing the songs, and after about 18 months I had made significant changes in my life.

I had secured full-time employment, a stable place to live and started to clear my debts. I had fallen in love and committed myself to a long-term relationship for the first time in my life. We had decided to go on a holiday together and we were excited about sharing this adventure, so we made the commitment to save the money needed. In a matter of months, we had enough money for our amazing holiday. That was about 25 years ago, and I can still recall the sense of joy and adventure I experienced on that holiday.

After the holiday, I realised that we had just saved $3,000 within a few months, so surely we could save $10,000 for a house deposit. I always dreamed of owning a home but thought that dream was

LET THE TREASURE HUNT BEGIN

well beyond what was possible for me. I could now imagine it as a reality, so I discussed it with my partner and we set our goal.

We started talking about it in January, thinking we would take 12 to 18 months to save the deposit. We researched the housing market. We met with the bank to learn about our lending capacity and we talked to our friends and workmates about it.

One of our workmates told us that she had just seen a sign for a "half-price house" and that we should go and have a look at it. With a high level of scepticism and curiosity, we went to find this sign, which actually read "house on half an acre". It was a little old house in the middle of the cane fields, and we loved it.

We talked about that house and focused on our savings. Within a few days, my boss called me over. She said to me, "This is how you will get your house. I am going to put $10,000 into your bank account, you ask your bank for a loan to buy that house plus $10,000 for home improvements and use that $10,000 to pay me back."

That's exactly what we did. We moved into our very own home only ten weeks after we made the decision to save a house deposit and we had put the $10,000 back into my boss's bank account only five weeks after she leant it to us.

Think about this in relation to the HYHM theory - Help You Help Me.

Through our words and actions, we helped my boss to feel comfortable to put this money into our bank account. She knew that we were trustworthy, reliable, and would understand the value of her offer. She also knew that we would do everything in our power to put the money back into her account as soon as we could. In return, my boss felt good because she helped us. She knew her gesture would have a significant impact on our quality of life for years to come, and it has.

I don't walk around in life believing that people should help me; in fact, I know that I am completely responsible for myself. I just stay open to the HYHM theory, and all manner of opportunities are presented to me. Later in this book, we will discuss how the HYHM theory creates a win/win situation for the giver and the receiver.

Thinking About the Past

Our past life experiences can lead us to believe that we cannot fulfil our dreams in life. This belief limits our future. Many people actually stop dreaming; they only have a vague idea of what they want. Even those who do have dreams don't take the next step to clarify their dream; it's this unclear thought in the back of their mind. They have never written it down and taken a good look at it. Some people might be clear about their dream, but they have never turned it into a goal, they haven't thought about how they will turn this dream into a reality. Then there are those who have set a goal with the action plan, but they still don't do the actions; they procrastinate, and nothing happens, so they give up. This procrastination is often the result of our fears and limiting beliefs.

Our past life experiences can result in us believing things that aren't true. We may not even know that we have these limiting false beliefs because they are buried in our unconscious mind.

LET THE TREASURE HUNT BEGIN

Given the opportunity to think about it, most people do have a rough idea of what they would like their life to be like.

You can use this book and the accompanying tools to help you clarify what you want in your life.

Three actions to get started on your Good Life Game Plan. I have included the instructions for each of these activities in the appendices.

1. Complete the **My Good Life** section
2. Write your **Letter to Me**
3. Do **My Dream Life Interview**

If you prefer, you can purchase the **Good Life Game Plan Pack** from www.thevillageleaders.com.au and be guided through all the activities mentioned in this book.

"We can't get what we want if we don't know what we want.

We can't know what we want if we don't make the space to think about it."

Jennifer Emmett

PART 2
Finding the Map

Unconscious[4]
Noun
The part of the mind which is inaccessible to the conscious mind but which affects behaviours and emotions.

What is Stopping You?

We have talked about the things that would make your life good, so what is stopping you from doing and having those things?

In my experience, most people have a rough idea of what they want in life and given the opportunity, they can learn how to clearly define their dreams. Then it is just a process of spending a few hours clarifying your current goals, preparing an action plan and doing the steps in the plan.

So why isn't everybody already living their good life or at least doing the steps to take them closer to their good life? Here are the four main reasons I have discovered over the years.

One: Limited Self Investment

I have discovered that a high majority of people I talk to don't allow themselves the time or put in the effort to clarify their own dreams.

Think about the ways you currently spend your time and money. What percentage of your time and money do you invest in becoming the person who lives the life you want for yourself?

If you dream about having a particular skill, what are you doing to learn that skill? Do you go to classes? Are you doing an online course? Do you watch free online content? I am constantly amazed by what I can learn for free if I just invest the time to find it and do the learning. I even discovered that through my local library eResources I can do online courses for free. Then there is TED Talks, YouTube, audio books and thousands of podcasts talking about topics that I want to learn more about. If I want to invest less time I can invest some money; there is usually someone out there who has already learnt the things that I want to know and I am happy to pay them to show me the shortcuts, tips and tricks that I need to know. I am happy to pay for that particular learning because I know a well-considered investment in myself will pay off over time. There is an avalanche of paid learning opportunities available these days, so I do make sure that I understand what I am paying for and that the provider is reputable. I also check-in with myself regarding my commitment to complete the learning. If I pay for training that does not support my goals or that I am not committed to completing, I am potentially wasting my time and money, so I ask myself questions like: Does this learning opportunity support my goals? Am I committed to completing this learning? Is this a good investment for the current and future me?

Two: False Goals

Some people do clarify their dreams, but the resulting goals are completely unrealistic and unachievable. They set goals that are not right for them. They set goals because someone of influence in their life (parents/teacher/partner/friend) wants them to do it. Sometimes people set goals to be or have something because they admire someone else. They fall into the trap of comparing themselves to others and thinking that if they were just like that person, they would be happy.

Let's take a look at my fictional friend, Lorna, for example. Lorna has started to think about her dreams and is ready to invest in herself. She knows she wants a good relationship with her family members, annual holiday travel adventures and a nice home.

Lorna looks around her and sees Rob, the dentist. Rob has a nice house, cars and a boat. He and his family go on two holidays each year and they look happy.

Lorna sets her goal to become a dentist, and she is excited about the possibilities. In the back of her mind, she kind of knows that she is not that interested in teeth and gums but that doesn't matter, she wants what Rob has.

She starts researching what it will take for her to become a dentist and she discovers that she has to obtain the required University Admissions Index Mark, then complete the Undergraduate Medicine and Health Sciences Admission Test, then complete a degree course in dentistry, then be registered with the Dental Board of Australia, and then complete a minimum of 60 hours of continuing professional development activities over a three-year cycle.

Phew….Lorna decides that she really does not want to be a dentist and she gives up on her goal and her dreams before she even gets started.

Luckily for Lorna, she very quickly discovered that she was not committed to her goal of becoming a dentist. She invested no money and very little time in this unsuitable goal. Some people do invest time and money only to discover later that it was not the right goal for them.

What goals could Lorna have set to achieve her dreams of having a good relationship with her family members, annual holiday travel adventures and a nice home? The possibilities are endless. It turned out that Lorna loved to learn and talk about cloud computing and within a few years she became qualified to design and deliver cloud computer courses. This allowed Lorna the freedom to often work from home, have time to spend with her family and generated the income she needed to have holidays and a nice home.

Three: No Plan

Some people do set the right goals for them, but then they don't know how to plan the achievable steps they will take to get there. The well-known author on personal time management, Alan Larkin said: "Failing to plan is planning to fail." So, if you set a goal and then do not make a plan to achieve that goal is it actually a goal or are you still dreaming?

Sometimes when I hear people talk about what they are going to do in their life, I think of that line delivered by the character, Darryl Kerrigan, played by Michael Caton, in the 1997 comedy The Castle. **"Tell 'em they're dreamin"!**

It's not that I don't believe that they could do it. It's just that when I ask them questions about how they are going to do it they have no idea; they have not made a plan and they haven't taken any actions towards it. A dream is not a goal until it has a plan.

Later in this book, you will learn how to turn your dreams into goals, or as I prefer to call them, **My Good Life Game Plans.**

Four: Self-Limiting Mindset

You may have been through the process of setting the right goal, creating your action plan, starting to do the actions on your plan and feeling really excited about it, and then you stop doing the actions on your plan.

You say to yourself things like:
- I will get back to that, I just need to do this other really important thing right now.
- I am not feeling motivated right now, I just need to wait until I get my mojo back.
- I am too busy at the moment, I will do it when I have more time.
- I will wait until the weather is better.
- Insert other good excuses here….

And then when you don't get back to it you say things like:
- That was not really that important to me.
- I don't care about that.
- It is someone or something else's fault.

Have you ever experienced a scenario like this?

Lorna decided that she wanted to be healthy.

She set her goal and made her plan for the next 90 days:
- Prepare a list of meals for the week.
- Buy the ingredients needed for the meals.
- On Sundays, spend time meal prepping so that it is easier during the week.
- Join the local gym.
- Go to the gym two mornings per week.
- Walk two afternoons per week.
- Park the car two blocks away from work.
- Make an appointment to get skin checked.

In the first week, she does most of the things on the list, and she feels great.

FINDING THE MAP

In the second week, she misses the gym sessions because she suddenly needed to go to work early. Also, she was just too busy to park the car and walk the two blocks.

In the third week, she did not plan her meals or buy the ingredients, meaning she could not do any meal prep, and she fell back into her old unhealthy eating habits. She never got around to booking her skin check even though there is a new brown mark that is slightly raised.

What happened to her dream of being healthy, her initial excitement and feeling good?

Let's have a closer look to see what is really going on here.

We humans have incredibly powerful minds. We have the ability to learn complex tasks and repeat those tasks over and over again. We constantly receive information about our surrounding environment and respond to this information. We can respond to things before we even know we are responding.

Have you ever had something slip out of your hand and caught it before it hit the ground? Have you ever avoided hitting the car in front of you when it unexpectedly stopped? Have you driven home from work and have no memory of the time between leaving work and pulling up in the driveway?

These types of things happen because we all have our very own automatic pilot. This automatic pilot is constantly on duty, monitoring our environment and ready to take action within a split second. Our autopilot is there to keep us safe and make sure our life stays on track.

This automatic pilot is more commonly referred to as our unconscious mind.

Like any automatic system, ours came with the necessary framework and some initial operating protocols. From the moment our life began, the system started to receive information so that it could develop and program the operating protocols specific to our life. It learned what our life looks like and what it needed to do to keep us on track. Our autopilot knows how to breathe, walk, talk, eat, brush our teeth, have a shower, button our shirt, tie our shoelaces, drive the car and all the other thousands of complex things we do each day.

Do you remember learning how to walk or tie your shoelaces? Do you remember learning how to drive a car? It seemed hard at first, and now we can do it without even thinking about it. This is because our automatic pilot/unconscious mind is an extremely powerful tool in our life, it does not judge us, it is just there to serve us as per the program and the operating protocols.

Then we also have our conscious mind; this is where we are aware of the things around us. We can choose to notice the things around us in our travels home from work. We can notice the things that we see, hear, smell, taste and feel on our journey and we can recall them from our short-term memory when we get home. This is called mindfulness or being present.

Through our life experiences, our unconscious mind may have programming and operating protocols that limit our ability to achieve the life we want for ourselves.

So, if we look back at Lorna's goal to be healthy, she failed to complete that goal because the actions she started to take were contradictory to the operating protocols of her autopilot. She could do it when her conscious mind had control, but when her conscious mind got distracted by her work, the autopilot kicked in and operated the other parts of her life. It followed the established program.

We know that there are chemical and physical changes that can occur in the brain resulting in reduced mental health. Although there may be a relationship between the programming of our unconscious mind and mental illness, the tools I discuss in this book are not designed to treat mental illness. If you are looking for professional support for mental illness, please contact a suitable GP or support service.

I am talking about the general self-doubt, self-sabotage, negative self-talk and resistance to change that we all experience at times in our life. Some of us experience this to a higher degree than others, but we all experience it. Whether we recognise it or not, we all experience some level of fear. It might be fear of change, fear of failure, fear of success, fear of being wrong, fear of being judged, fear of standing out, fear of saying the wrong thing, fear of someone disagreeing with us, and all the other fears we feel. This fear can stop us from taking actions to fulfil our dreams.

Another thing that many people do is constantly look back to what happened in the past. Their body might be here in the present, but their mind is stuck in the past. They replay past events over and over in their unconscious mind, they talk about it to anyone who will listen, and they never let it go, they never move onto their current life.

How can you look forward to the life that you want for yourself if you are constantly looking back at the life you don't want for yourself? It is like walking around with your head turned back to see where you have been rather than looking forward to seeing where you are now and where you are going next. We all need to spend some time to process the things that happen in our life, and then we need to find a way to accept it and move on.

Have you ever met a person who is stuck in the past? They cannot accept something that has happened in their life. They will often say things like "life is unfair" or "nothing good ever happens". They may unconsciously believe that their life can never change.

Tools to Find Your Good Life

Let's have a look at some of the tools you can use to consciously re-write your programs so that your autopilot does the things that will create the life you want for yourself.

Our mind is working all the time from the moment we wake to the moment we sleep, and then when we sleep our unconscious mind is still working on things for us.

If you get seven to eight hours of sleep each night, you are awake between sixteen to seventeen hours each and every day. That's 57,600 to 61,200 seconds of thinking time per day. We know that our thoughts can be fleeting and many thoughts can seem to cross our minds at once. We have tens of thousands of thoughts every day and many of them can loop over and over; they are there reconfirming our program so that our autopilot knows how to respond to any given situation.

Do you know the types of thoughts that you have? What are the thinking loops that play in your mind? What programs are you setting and reconfirming for yourself?

Here is a broad overview of the steps you can take to change your autopilot's programming. You will have the opportunity to learn more about these steps as you read through this book and do the accompanying activities.

Step One - What Am I Thinking?
Step one is to start understanding what we actually think about. We are so good at unconsciously thinking our thoughts that our conscious mind doesn't even know what these thoughts are. If we want to re-program our autopilot we need to know which parts of the program no longer serve us. When we regularly and consciously ask ourselves, what am I thinking, we can start to learn about our unconscious thoughts.

If we ask this question with curiosity and non-judgment we can observe ourselves and learn about the thoughts that are holding us back.

I call this process **W.A.I.T** and I regularly remind myself to **W.A.I.T**. I have cards with the letters W.A.I.T and a question mark on them. You can write **W.A.I.T?** on sticky notes and stick them in places where you will have a few seconds to ask yourself this question and consciously take notice of the things you are thinking about.

Stick them in your car, on your bedroom door, on the bathroom mirror - any place where you are doing mundane, routine things. You might be surprised by what you learn about your unconscious thoughts.

You might discover that you have thoughts that you would prefer not to have. Don't worry about it. There is no need to ever judge our thoughts; just observing them and learning how to replace less helpful thoughts with more helpful thoughts can change your life.

Step Two - Write My New Program
Step two is to write your new program - write your preferred reality scripts to match your dreams, personal vision, goals and action plans.

Step Three - Install My New Program
Step three is to start installing your new program. Your old program has been in place for a long time; it often dates back to your childhood or experiences you had as a young adult. It's a well-worn neural pathway and your autopilot knows all the operational protocols. Now that you want to create new neural pathways, it will take time and effort to build these new paths and you might find your autopilot regularly slipping you back over to the old habits - the habits that keep you trapped in the life you do not want for yourself. Don't despair when this happens; over time your autopilot will learn the new program. You just need to keep exposing it to the new you, use your preferred reality scripts and get back to doing the actions in your **Good Life Game Plan**.

Step Four - Observe the Results
Monitor and observe your life and yourself over time to see what is changing to your preferred reality, what is not changing and what is changing in ways you did not expect.

I have used the words autopilot, programming, and operating protocols to help me explain the unconscious mind. I am talking about the things we have seen and experienced in our past and the conscious and unconscious beliefs we have developed through these past experiences. Another way to explain this is that through our past experiences we have created a set of beliefs, and these beliefs are often buried in our unconscious mind and limit our current and future options in life. If we can change our mind, we can change our life.

FINDING THE MAP

We know we can change our minds - we often see examples of this done in negative and destructive ways - we call it brainwashing. It has been used in warfare, religious cults, unhealthy relationships and one could argue that much of the advertising we are exposed to daily is designed to make us believe that we really need something.

In this book we discuss how you can use this knowledge in a positive way, to consciously change your beliefs and behaviours in ways that you control and that support you to create the life that you want for yourself.

Three actions to become more conscious of our unconscious thoughts:

1. **Learn to regularly ask yourself, What Am I Thinking? W.A.I.T?**

    You can write it on sticky notes and put them up where you will regularly ask yourself, What Am I Thinking?

2. **Remind yourself why you started**

    Have another look at your **Letter to Me**.

3. **Get a better understanding of your dreams**

    Review your **Dream Life Interview** and consider if your thoughts match your dream life.

"Our actions and sometimes our non-actions will cause reactions. Our actions are often habitual being created by the beliefs we established through our past experiences. If we can change our beliefs, we can change our habitual actions and change our lives."

Jennifer Emmett

PART 3

Adventure Bound

Belief[4]

Noun

1. An acceptance that something exists or is true, especially one without proof.
2. (belief in) Trust, faith, or confidence in (someone or something).

You may have heard of the term self-sabotage. You may have even observed other people sabotaging their relationships, career, financial security, health and wellbeing. You may have seen other people doing things to create problems in their life or stop themselves from achieving their own much-desired goals.

You may have observed people engage in common methods of self-sabotage, including procrastination, saying or doing things that will have undesirable consequences, self-medication with drugs or alcohol, comfort eating, and self-harm.

The fact is, at times we all engage in activities that reduce our quality of life. Most people have no idea why they do it; some people don't even know that they are doing it to themselves. You may be able to identify when someone else is engaging in self-sabotage but not see when you are doing it to yourself. Sometimes you may realise that you are doing it but can't find a way to stop it.

Many years ago, I came to understand that things were going wrong in my life because of my own thoughts, feelings, words and actions. I then blamed myself and felt guilty for thinking, feeling, saying and doing these things. In my mind, I was less of a person because I could not maintain a relationship. I was less of a person because I drank too much alcohol. I was less of a person because I maintained an emotional distance from most people. I was less of a person because I ate the wrong food. I was less of a person because I was overweight. I was less of a person because I did not look the right way. The less of a person list continued. While it was a good step for me to understand that I was fully responsible for what was going on in my life, I eventually come to understand that there is only ever one good time to engage in blame and that time is NEVER.

Engaging in blame and guilt will only ever lead to attracting more of the stuff we don't want in our life. I realised that I needed to learn more and re-think this whole self-sabotage concept because my current beliefs were not helping me live my good life.

I learnt more about how our unconscious mind works and the analogy that our brain is like a computer with a programmed autopilot that steps up and operates our life when we are not consciously on duty. I then understood that I was not less of a person; my autopilot was just operating as per the program. I did not need to blame myself, I did not need to feel guilty, I just needed to learn more about my operating program and tweak it to get the outcomes that were more desirable to me.

I stopped thinking about self-sabotage and I started to think about my program. I changed from a self-blame, guilt, self-judgement mentality to looking at my program with curiosity, wonder and non-judgement. I learnt the power of being kind to myself.

When I say the word program, I am really talking about our beliefs. The beliefs that we have consciously and unconsciously established throughout our life. Previously we discussed how our past life experiences influence our current beliefs, and now we will think about how our beliefs impact our thoughts, feelings, words and actions.

Our thoughts, feelings, words and actions create reactions, and I draw your attention to this popular quote which is often attributed to Mahatma Gandhi but is rumoured to have been around for so long that the original source is unclear.

Keep your thoughts positive because your thoughts become your words
Keep your words positive because your words become your behaviours
Keep your behaviours positive because your behaviours become your habits
Keep your habits positive because your habits become your values
Keep your values positive because your values become your destiny.

If we don't think about our current beliefs, we will not be able to understand how they are impacting our thoughts, feelings, words and actions.

If we want our life to change, we need to change. We need to change our beliefs, which in turn will change our thoughts, feelings, words and actions. Once we change our thoughts, feelings, words and actions, we will see different reactions. When we learn to use our thoughts, feelings, words and actions wisely we can start getting the reactions we want, and we can start to live our preferred reality.

Many people I talk to don't know how to change their beliefs. In fact, they refuse to even consider it an option and they continue to live a life they do not want.

Most people can identify the things they don't like about their life, but they are stuck in a blaming mindset. They blame themselves or others for the things they don't like about their life. When I consciously made the decision to learn how to let go of blame I started to open my mind to change and new opportunities. I also took the time to understand and accept my current reality and planned for my preferred reality.

You will see people all around you who do not accept their current reality. You will know them because they will be saying things like; "I shouldn't have to," "It isn't fair," "I can't stand this," "This can't be true," "It shouldn't be this way".

Here is an example of non-acceptance of reality.

I worked as the CEO of an affordable housing company for ten years. I have worked with property investors, tenants and all levels of government. Through these ten years, our region experienced an economic boom and bust cycle. Many of the property investors bought their rental property based on their belief that the boom would continue with an ever-increasing amount of rental income. When the rental market crashed and the vacancy rate changed from .07% to over 9%, rents dropped by $100 to $150 per week. I myself reduced the rent on my investment property by $135 per week, and the value of my portfolio dropped by $180,000.

Our company provided the property investors with information and data about why it was in their best interest to reduce their rent to stay competitive in an oversupplied rental market.

The ones who refused to reduce the rent to match this new reality did not retain their tenants and could not secure new tenants. Some of these investors took six to twelve months to reduce the rent and they lost thousands of dollars due to this inability to accept this new reality. Although most property investors in our region were impacted by this reduction in demand, the people who refused to accept this new reality experienced more financial hardship and distress than they needed to. They blamed others for their vacant property, loss of income and unsustainable financing modelling. They continued to make decisions not accepting their current reality, resulting in continued hardship and distress.

Although I recognise that I now have a very good life, there have been times when I was not making good decisions and not living the life I wanted. I have experienced depression, separation from myself and others, negative self-talk and blame, and for many years I experienced regular thoughts of suicide.

When I learnt to accept my current reality and see life's challenges as opportunities, I started to move towards my preferred reality. I don't see this concept of preferred reality as an end destination. I see it as a way that I live my life. I continue to develop my skills of self-observation and adjustment. I accept that life will still send some challenges my way and I aim to be able to recognise the opportunities contained within these challenges.

We can develop our ability to know when to accept and adjust and when to not accept something in our life. We can learn to pick our battles wisely and not turn life into a constant fight that we never win.

When we develop the ability to know that our autopilot is steering us into the dark, mind-numbing hole of blame, we can start to avoid the belief that people or things are conspiring against us or that life is not fair or good.

This takes practice and persistence, and in this book, I am sharing with you some tools to help you along this journey of understanding and accepting your current reality, identifying your preferred reality and reprogramming your autopilot (your unconscious mind) with protocols that match your preferred reality.

Now, we will discuss the ABCDE model of feelings and actions. You will learn about actions and reactions. We will look at a blaming mindset versus the acceptance of reality, and we will consider if there is another way to think about your past.

The ABCDE Of Our Feelings and Actions

Think about driving in your car during peak hour traffic. Are you feeling calm and relaxed? Are you enjoying your trip to your destination, taking in the sights, sounds, smells around you, perhaps listening to some music or a podcast or using this time to be mindful, or are you having a stressful and even aggressive journey?

Our friend Lorna does not have a calm and relaxed trip to work each day. Although Lorna is generally a nice person, for some reason she often finds herself swearing or using negative language at the people in the vehicles around her. She regularly feels annoyed because someone cut her off or braked all of a sudden, or the traffic is too slow, or the person in front of her took too long to get onto the roundabout.

Lorna often waves her arms in frustration telling the other drivers they are idiots.

She shakes her head, wondering why she has to deal with this s*#t every day.

By the time she gets to work, she is highly annoyed. She walks in and tells her colleagues about the horrible person who cut her off and that they ruined her day. Now she feels so annoyed, how is she supposed to work after that...could this day get any worse?

I am constantly amazed at how many (usually nice) people have negative trips in their car. There are some people I will not be a passenger with because their level of aggression is so high, or they are so rude to the other drivers.

The ABCDE model developed by Psychologist Albert Ellis is briefly explained below.
A Stands for **A**ctivating Event or adversity
B Stands for **B**elief
C Stands for Emotional and Behavioral **C**onsequence
D Stands for **D**isputes or arguments against the belief
E Stands for New **E**ffect/Emotions and behaviours in response to **A**

Many people think that **A** creates **C**. That is, an event happens and I have an emotional and behavioural response to that activating event.

Let's have a think about what is going on for Lorna in relation to the ABCDE model.

Lorna's **A**ctivating event is:
Someone cut her off in traffic.

Her **C**onsequences are:
Lorna felt annoyed.

She waves her arms in the air, says mean things about the other drivers, says, "they ruined my day," tells her colleagues about it and is distracted from her work.

It is more accurate to say that **A+B** creates **C**.

Let's have another look at what is going on for Lorna.
Activating Event
Someone cut her off in traffic.

Beliefs
Lorna believes that they cut her off on purpose or they are all idiots who should not be allowed on the road and that she should just have a traffic-free trip to work.

Consequences
Lorna feels annoyed.
She waves her arms in the air, says mean things about the other drivers, says, "they ruined my day," tells her colleagues about it and is distracted from her work.

What would the consequence be if Lorna Disputed or argued her own beliefs?

What if she decided to **Believe**.... they may not have seen me, and I only needed to apply the brakes for a split second to avoid hitting them, it's no big deal. Things don't always run smoothly in traffic and I am responsible for being observant of the drivers around me. It could just as easily be me who cuts someone off.

Do you think that Lorna would feel annoyed and that her day was ruined if she had these different beliefs when someone cut her off in traffic? Is it more likely that she would just feel a moment of relief that she noticed the other driver and avoided a collision and then pretty much forgot about it and moved on with her day?

If she Disputes and changes her **Belief** she would end up with different Effect/Emotions and behaviours in response to **A**.

When we understand that it is our beliefs that cause our feelings and actions, we can intervene. We can change our beliefs (reprogram our unconscious mind) which will change our thoughts, feelings, words and actions.

Actions and reactions

To every action, there is always opposed an equal reaction
Isaac Newton

You will often hear people talk about choices and consequences, which in other words are actions and reactions.

Although we cannot know for sure what the reactions to our actions or our non-actions will be, we can stack the odds in our favour.

In the driving scenario discussed above, Lorna's actions will have created reactions.

Lorna waving her arms in the air and abusing the other driver may have resulted in a reaction from the other driver. They may have abused her in return and in a worst-case scenario they may have engaged in road rage, resulting in physical injury to Lorna.

Lorna regularly walking into work and complaining to her colleagues may mean that they start to avoid her because they think she is a negative whinger. If she often gets distracted from her work due to feelings of annoyance she will not do her best work and her employer may have cause to raise concern with her about her quality of work, and if it continues she may lose her job.

Here is one of my personal examples. If my actions involve eating lots of sugary and high carb food, the odds are that I will put on weight, my knee joints become painful, I will feel back pain and I will snore. I will find it harder to do physical activity and I will be more prone to feelings of depression. I won't fit into my clothes and I will have increased my risk of diabetes, heart disease and certain cancers.

I don't want any of those reactions in my life, so the simple solution is to take different actions - limit my intake of sugary and high carb foods, eat fresh fruits and vegetables, reduce processed foods, and generally reduce the amount of food I consume.

Of course, this sounds like a simple solution because it is a simple solution. But if you are like me and have struggled with an addiction to using food to manage your emotions, you will know that it is often not easy to resist the urge to comfort eat.

Like any habitual addiction, there are underlying reasons why we started the habit and it has become a part of our program to eat more than we need. We know that we already feel full, but we still want to eat more food. For many years I tried to outsource the responsibility for ensuring I ate a healthy amount of food. I had this vague thinking that some person (unknown to me) would arrange all my healthy meals for me. When I came to the understanding and accepted that I was responsible for my healthy eating and drinking, I found a whole new level of ability to change my habits. I set my goal, made a commitment to myself, wrote my healthy life scripts and created my health song. We will discuss preferred reality scripts and life songs later in the book. My health song is very upbeat, and I enjoyed dancing and singing it. My health song reminds me to take the actions that I had committed to. I also knew that actively singing this song was reprogramming my autopilot and that over time I would no longer have such strong cravings for food and drinks that were not good for me.

When I wrote my health song, I had not planned to give up or even cut back on my alcohol consumption, but it turned out that putting alcohol in my body was contradictory to the words of my song. Although I had often enjoyed a drink or two and in my younger days had an unhealthy relationship with alcohol, it made me feel unwell after just two or three drinks and the next morning I had less focus and energy.

Within a few weeks of writing my preferred health script and turning it into my health song, I had created a new belief and my autopilot started to take actions to remove my consumption of alcohol. I remember the first time it happened; I was cooking dinner and having a drink at the same time. I went to the freezer to get some ice for a second drink and a thought popped into my head. My autopilot was telling me that I would really enjoy that ice in a big glass of water, so I put the ice in water, and I did enjoy it. I also felt much better in the morning, so I decided I would just keep enjoying water.

I am not saying that writing a preferred reality script and turning it into a song is the cure for addiction, but perhaps it is one of the tools you can put in your tool kit.

In this example, my actions were to make a decision to put food and drinks in my body that were good for me, write my health goal and commit to it, write my preferred reality scripts and create a song to match this decision, regularly sing my health song, and do the things I said I was going to do.

The reactions that I had planned for were; that I lost weight, my body felt better, and I improved my long-term health. I did not know that I would choose to significantly reduce my consumption of alcohol but, I am happy with that unplanned reaction.

> "*Our actions and sometimes our non-actions will cause reactions. Our actions are often habitual being created by the beliefs we established through our past experiences. If we can change our beliefs, we can change our habitual actions and change our lives.*"
>
> — Jennifer Emmett

Blaming Mindset vs Acceptance

> *Discontent, blaming, complaining, self-pity cannot serve as a foundation for a good future, no matter how much effort you make.*
>
> — Eckhart Tolle

Every day we see things happen in the world that can cause feelings of pain, loss and grief. We see natural disasters like cyclones, floods and bushfires, we see domestic violence, we see war, we see crime and people who have become dependent on drugs, alcohol, food, sex, self-harm, cigarettes etc. to try and manage their emotions. We see animal abuse and desecration of our natural environment. We see death, illness, disability and destruction all around us, and sometimes these things are happening to us.

It can be easy to get stuck in the belief that life is bad, and we can blame others or ourselves for the things that happen around or to us. Every time we play the blame game we are doing ourselves a disservice; we are programming our autopilot with the message that life is bad and that ourselves and others are responsible for this bad. Our autopilot will follow this operational protocol of attracting bad things to our life. On the other hand, we can accept that things happen, knowing that we judge events in our life based on our own beliefs which have been formed through our past experiences.

There are some things we can change and there are some things we cannot change.

Reinhold Niebuhr's Serenity Prayer sums it up very well - *God, grant me the serenity to accept the things I cannot change, courage to change the things I can, and wisdom to know the difference.*

We do not need to conform to everything that happens in our life, there are lots of things we can influence, we just need to pick our battles wisely.

We may be able to influence the world through protest or becoming a community or political leader, we may be able to influence what happens in our home environment through our words and actions. We do have the power to change many things in our lives and then there are some things we cannot change or that are not important enough for us to make a significant effort and commitment to change.

One of my dearest and closest friends experienced many years of illness and eventually passed away. I could not make her well, but I could spend time with her. I cannot bring her back, but I can accept that she is no longer alive and no longer suffering. I can honour her memory and be grateful for her love and friendship over many years. I can still talk to her and have a pretty good idea of what she would say back to me, and I can keep living my good life.

If you believe your parents or someone else mistreated you when you were a child, you cannot change what they did. You can choose to accept that the past happened and know that the past is not your now or your future. If you continue to blame people for their past actions, you will remain a victim who is stuck in the past.

Forgiveness is much better for ourselves than being stuck in blame. In fact, I have come to the understanding that I have no need to forgive anyone because having the need to forgive would mean I was engaging in blame. I prefer to focus on the actions that match my preferred reality.

In relation to the addiction to comfort eating and how that created reactions that I did not want in my life, the last thing I needed to do was blame myself for the action of overeating. I needed to be kind to myself because negative self-talk is the very thing that would see me standing with the fridge door open looking for something sweet in an effort to suppress my feelings of distress or inadequacy.

You Can't Change Your Past, Or Can You?

You know that saying, you can't change your past, and for the most part that is true, but think about this. Your understanding of your past is your mind's version of what happened. Your mind will have retained some of the facts and it will fill the gaps based on your beliefs. There are always numerous versions of the same events; there is what you think happened, what others think happened and what actually happened.

One of my childhood memories is when at six years old, I was taken from my family, put on a train and sent to a Bush Children's Home for six weeks. I remember being in a strange place with strange people, and I was very scared. I remember a girl stole my ruler and when I asked for it back she said that it was hers. I pointed out that it had my name on it and she said that was her sister's name, and I did not know how to respond to that. I believe I never got my ruler back, but perhaps I did. I remember being sick and laying up in the dorm room all alone while there was singing downstairs. I wanted to be involved in the singing, but I did not want to be with all those scary kids.

At six years old I was shy and easily bullied. I also struggled to understand the concepts that the teachers were trying to teach in class. The teacher would write things on the blackboard for us to copy into our exercise books but when I looked down to write in the book and then looked back at the blackboard, I struggled to find the next word to write. I had lost my place and things moved too quickly for me to keep up. My family tells me that I went through a stage of running away from school (we lived in the same street as the school) and the local police officer, who was also located close to the school, would escort me back to class. I don't remember that, but I do remember my Grade 1 teacher dragging me out of the classroom by my left earlobe because I could not read the date and time. In my memory, I honestly had no idea how to make sense of those marks on the blackboard, but she seemed to believe that I was purposely not doing what she told me to do. Not long after that, I was sent to the Bush Children's Home.

For many years when I thought about my past, that girl who was clearly not smart enough because she got taken from her family and sent to a strange place. She was the daughter of an alcoholic father, the one who struggled to understand what the school teachers were talking about, the one who had difficulty learning how to write and spell, the one who always came last in races, the one who always felt like an outsider. I rejected this child and her fears until eventually,

I understood that in rejecting her I was rejecting myself. Today I carry that innocent child who struggled to understand a confusing world and my heart swells with love for her.

Now in my memories I, the adult who loves her, am always there with her, telling her that she is ok, that these experiences are making her the person she will become.

I am there on the train with her.
I am in the dorm room with her.
I am in the classroom smiling at her.
I am with her every time her father came home drunk.
I am sitting on her bed while her father starts the chainsaw in the kitchen and threatens to chop up her family.
I am there through her teenage years reminding her that she will get through it and it is worth living.
I am there with her when the older girls are bullying her at work.
I am there when she makes mistakes in life, reminding her that she is learning how to be the person she wants to be.

I am always there, through every phase of her life. The past still happened, but I no longer have fear, sadness or regret about it. I do not feel like I was alone; I have love and gratitude for my past experiences and respect for the younger me who walked a path that led me to an amazingly good life.

Your autopilot is a very effective tool to keep you safe and keep your life on track. It is working for you right now. If the information you are reading in this book is vastly contradictory to your current program, your autopilot will be giving you thoughts and feelings that resist this information. It may even create distractions in your life so that you don't continue to read this book. This is often referred to as resistant to change, and we all do it. The thing is, if we want our life to change, we need to change. You can use your conscious mind to consider new information and make conscious decisions about what changes you want in your life.

If you are currently blaming someone or something else for the way your life is or if you have not yet accepted responsibility for your own beliefs, thoughts, feelings, words and actions, your autopilot might be saying statements like, "that's just the way I am" or "I can't change because…" "This is not true" "It's not my fault that…" "It is my fault that…."

These statements are not true; they are just your autopilot working to keep your life on the known path. These statements come from our resistance to change and our fear of being different to who we are now. We do not need to blame ourselves for having this resistance to change or fear, but if we want to create our preferred reality, we do need to make conscious decisions about what changes we want in our lives and do it anyway. If we let our resistance to change and fear control our life, we will never move beyond our current reality. Change is possible; you don't have to do it all at once, in fact, it is often best to do it one small step at a time.

I find it very helpful to answer the questions in the ABCDE model when I am feeling distressed about events that are happening in my life.

I like to use questions relevant to my preferred life to capture my thinking and feelings as they happen, so I design my own online forms and place links on my phone. That way I can easily fill them out when I need to. I have created the **ABCDE of My Feelings and Actions** Google Forms Template and Microsoft Forms Template. If you are comfortable using online forms, they are a great way to capture and process your thinking and feelings on the fly. I have also created a PDF version for those who prefer to use printed forms.

You can download your free copies of the **ABCDE of My Feelings and Actions** from www.thevillageleaders.com.au.

Three actions to learn more about changing your own thoughts, feelings, words and actions:

1. **Spend a little bit of time on the internet to learn more about the ABCDE Model.**
   If you have a copy of the **Good Life Game Plan** companion manual, check out the section on **Mastering My Thoughts, Feelings, Words and Actions.**

2. **Do some test runs on the ABCDE Model.**
   Over the coming days and weeks look for opportunities to test the model on yourself.
   A great time to test it is when you are feeling a little uncomfortable or upset about something that was done or said.

3. **Allow yourself to be open to the possibility that you could change your mind about something.** If we can change our mind, we can change our life.

"If you are searching for that one person that will change your life, take a look in the mirror."

Unknown

PART 4

Surprising Discoveries

Lost[4]
Adjective
1. Unable to find one's way; not knowing one's whereabouts.
2. That has been taken away or cannot be recovered.
3. (of a game or contest) in which a defeat has been sustained.

At the start of this book, I encouraged you to ask yourself these questions:
- What would make my life good?
- What would I be like?
- What would I do?
- What would I have?

Did you have clearly defined answers for those questions? Do you currently know who you want to be?

What sorts of things does the person you want to be, think, say, do and have? Are you that person right now or can you see yourself being that person? Do you feel like you have found you or are you feeling a little bit lost?

Thousands of people feel lost every day. We may feel lost for a minute, hours, days or weeks. We can feel lost in traffic, we can feel lost when we are walking busy streets, and we can also feel lost in our own life, with some people feeling this way for years.

Occasionally I meet someone who says they don't mind feeling lost and like being out of their comfort zone, but the majority of us find it distressing. We feel a great sense of relief when we are back in familiar territory. It is easy to understand that when we try to steer our life in different directions we find ourselves slipping back into old habits.

Even though our conscious mind knows we want change in our life, our autopilot kicks into emergency mode. It starts sending us all these warning messages telling us we are in unfamiliar territory - get back, get back, it might not be safe, we don't know about this, get out of there.

Did you ever watch the original Lost in Space TV series? The robot regularly said things like "Warning Warning Will Robinson", "Danger Will Robinson", "No Will Robinson". At the same time, the robot's chest would flash red and the music was dramatic.

Imagine trying to make a change in your life if you had that robot following you around and giving you dramatic warnings each time you wanted to do something unfamiliar. Well, you kind of do, it's your unconscious mind, so we can often feel a sense of distress when we are in unfamiliar places or situations. Sometimes we let that sense of distress take control of us and we decide to just stick to what we know even if we don't like it.

There are ways we can make it easier for ourselves to stick with the changes we want to make. We can reduce the level of warnings and distress by giving our unconscious mind advanced knowledge about where we are heading and what we will see along the way.

Here is one of my personal examples of how we can make it easier to stick with the changes.

My health goal includes increased physical activity, so I look for any small opportunities to increase my movement, knowing that lots of small changes add up to big results. I recently flew to Brisbane for a work meeting and my preferred reality is that I catch the Airtrain to the city and walk to my meeting destination. This recent meeting was not in the city; it was in a part of Brisbane that I had never been to. Also, there were health warnings on the radio telling people to stay inside due to the high level of smoke pollution from bushfires.

My autopilot started to signal warnings - danger, you better catch a cab from the airport and go directly to the meeting. My autopilot's response was due to a fear of the unknown. It did not know if there was a train station within walking distance of the meeting venue or how to get from a train station to the meeting venue. It did not know how long it would take me to drag my luggage to the venue. It did not know if I had enough time to walk there. It did not know how bad the smoke pollution would be. These were all very good excuses for me to not walk and gave me strong justification to just jump in a cab rather than sticking to my goal of increasing my daily movement.

The thing is, the cab option represented the behaviour of the person I did not want to be. I wanted to be the person who would catch a train from the airport and walk to the meeting venue. I wanted to be the person who took opportunities to fit movement into her daily routine because I know that moving my body is good for my health and my goal is to be healthy now and into the future.

I realised that my autopilot's response of just catching a cab would mean I was slipping back into old familiar habits. I really wanted to change my daily movement habits, but I was feeling distressed by all the warnings.

I spent a few minutes researching my options. I looked up the trains and discovered there was a station within walking distance. I looked at online maps and although the route out of the train station was not completely clear, I saw images of the buildings and landmarks that I would see when walking to the venue.

I decided that I would take the train and walk. If I got there and the smoke was really bad, I would just call a cab. See the breakdown of my journey and how my autopilot responded.

Leg of Journey	Familiarity	Autopilot Response	Conscious thinking/action
Home to Airport	Known	No Warnings	NA
Flight	Known	No Warnings	NA
Airport to Airtrain	Known	No Warnings	NA

SURPRISING DISCOVERIES

Disembark at train station	Somewhat Known	Minor warnings	Knew it was the right station because I had researched it
	Unfamiliar	Medium distress	Did not know how to exit the station and what direction to walk. Follow the crowd out and check the signs
			Could not smell smoke
Walking to venue	Unfamiliar	Minor warnings	Find a street sign
		Medium distress	Check Google maps
	Somewhat Known	Medium distress	Recheck Google maps and confirm direction
	Known	Minor distress	Seeing buildings and landmarks that I had seen on street view maps
			I know I am heading in the right direction and I know where I am going

Arriving at venue	Unfamiliar	Sense of achievement	I found my way
			I supported my health goal
		Relief	I have enough time
			I arrived safely
	Familiar	Confident	I know some of the people I will see as I find my way to the meeting room

There are many tools to help your autopilot become familiar with the changes you want to make in your life.

If we are unhappy with some aspect of our life and want it to be different, we need to know what that difference is, what it looks like, what it feels like. We need to research and make a plan of how we will get there, and we need to give ourselves signs and landmarks to know we are heading in the right direction. We also need to make conscious decisions and conscious actions to ensure we stick with it.

Our autopilot will send us warning messages and it will try to steer us back to what it knows. We will feel a level of distress and we will find lots of valid and powerful excuses to not make the changes we want in our life. We will be tempted to give up, engage in blame and stay stuck in a life we don't want.

We can reduce our autopilot's warning messages by providing it with information about our preferred reality. We can make conscious decisions to override our autopilot. We can choose to stick with

SURPRISING DISCOVERIES

the change even when we feel a level of distress. We can use every small achievement to build our confidence, knowing that life gets pretty exciting on the outer edge of our comfort zone.

In the example about my trip to Brisbane, I found it reasonably easy to get to my destination because I had done my research, made a plan, identified some landmarks and knew which signs to look out for. Even though I had never been there, I had a map and images in my mind of what I would see along the way.

You can successfully travel to the WHO you want to be by doing the research, making your plans, identifying the landmarks and signs and showing your mind what it will see along the way. Your research is undertaking activities to clarify in your own mind what would make life good for you and learning about your dreams. The planning is picking which dreams you want to turn into reality, clarifying that particular dream in detail, describing why that dream is important to you and making an action plan to achieve it. Your personal vision and the goals you set in your **Good Life Game Plan** will be your compass to guide your direction. In Part 6, we will discuss all the tools you can use to establish your maps, your signs and your landmarks.

Firstly, you will set your personal vision, because if we don't set a personal vision that matches the person we really want to be, we can spend our time, money and effort on things that don't support us to become that person. I have met people who chase material success and/or power over others, but they cannot name the things that give them a true sense of fulfilment. I have also met people who do not understand the power of their thoughts or their intent and they wonder why negative things keep happening to them.

Let's think about the types of things that truly bring fulfilment to your life. We will talk about the power of intent and how to say no to things that do not serve you. You will learn how to create your own personal vision.

It's Never Too Late to Create Your Personal Vision

My now wife and I performed as a music duo named Pelican Zen for many years. I remember a number of years ago we had been asked to play at the opening of an art exhibition. After the performance, we stayed around to socialise, and I got talking to a gentleman who had recently retired from a career in banking and bank management. He asked me if I made my living from music performance. I explained that it was a part-time hobby and I did it because I enjoyed it. At the time I was working as the Business Development Manager for two sister organisations; one supported people with a disability to gain and maintain employment and the other was a recycling centre. He seemed interested so I discussed some of the projects I had been working on.

Somewhere in the conversation, he said these words to me, "I wish I had understood this when I was younger, you are really doing it, I have spent my whole career focused on making money, I could have done so much more for people, instead I've lost my family, I'm retired and now what?"

Here was a highly-skilled man who had ended up without his family and not knowing what to do with the rest of his life.... I hope he did find a new purpose in his retirement years, but some people don't.

SURPRISING DISCOVERIES

At the end of the day money, power over others and material possessions do not bring us a sense of fulfilment in life. We do need money to pay for the things we need, and it is ok to buy nice things but if our pursuit of money and material possessions gets more of our attention than the other important things in life, we may end up feeling that our life has no purpose.

Over the years I have read many books about spirituality and self-awareness to understand my beliefs and practices. I have also read books in leadership and management. It struck me a few years ago that it did not matter if I was reading a spiritual book or a leadership book, the same message was coming up over and over again. The people who had achieved a level of skill and success in their spiritual development and/or leadership journey all seemed to understand this same thing. In one way or another, they were all sending this message. If you want to feel a true sense of fulfilment in your life, you need to know in your own heart and mind, that what you are doing is also good for others.

Think about this… we all have our unconscious mind/autopilot guiding our unconscious thoughts, feelings, words and actions based on its programming.

If we want to change the programming, we need to consciously say and do things that teach it the new program.

When we say and do things that are not good for others, we are reinforcing our autopilot's programming in a way that is not good for us. We might be programming or reinforcing the program that we are a liar, a thief, a violent or abusive person, a manipulative or controlling person, or that we are cowardly, cruel, cynical, defensive, devious, disloyal, disorganised, disrespectful, evasive, evil, foolish, forgetful, frivolous, weak, useless, fussy, gossipy, greedy, selfish, unlikeable or grumpy.

Do any of those character traits excite and inspire you to feel good about yourself? Would you really feel a sense of fulfilment in life if you consciously or unconsciously believed any of those things about yourself?

Your conscious mind can easily choose to not observe your words and actions, even the words and actions that you would consider to be negative or bad if someone else did it. This is called a lack of self-awareness. The thing is, your unconscious mind sees it all; it does not judge you, it just takes in the information and works to manage your life based on the program.

When we say and do things that are good for others, we are reinforcing our autopilot's programming in a way that is good for us. We might be programming or reinforcing the program with things like we are honest, generous, good-natured, respectful, considerate, brave, caring, open-minded, wise, loyal, organised, sincere, trustworthy, intelligent, dependable, understanding, thoughtful, reliable, warm, kind, friendly, unselfish, reasonable, likeable, patient, courageous or ethical.

Would you prefer to identify with character traits from this second list or the first list?

Here's the catch - you can't just pretend that you are saying or doing things that are good for others because your unconscious mind always knows exactly what you are thinking, it knows your true intent and it operates based on that programming.

SURPRISING DISCOVERIES

When you can learn how to say and do things that are good for others, knowing in your own heart and mind that your intention is good, you will start to change your program, you will start to understand more positive things about yourself, and you will be on the path of purpose and fulfilment.

This does not mean that you need to go and make dramatic changes in your personal or work life. You can start by looking for small opportunities to send your autopilot positive messages about yourself.

- Give that person the opportunity to turn off the side street into busy traffic
- Hold the door open for someone
- Donate goods, time or money to a charity
- Smile at people and say hello
- Do the dishes, take the bins out, cook dinner, clean the house (even though it is not your turn)
- Donate blood
- Pick up rubbish on the beach
- Say something nice about a person that others are gossiping about
- Send flowers just because you can
- Compliment others
- Give another person a job opportunity
- The possibilities are endless.

When Giving Is Not Really Giving

It is important to think about how and when we do things for others, so we support them to learn and shine in their own way.

Have you ever had someone insist on giving or doing something for you even though you really did not want them to and now you are stuck with it? Have you ever seen someone say or do things with good intentions, but they were actually being quite disrespectful towards the person they had intended to help?

Doing things with the intention of "fixing" others or trying to control or micromanage someone else's life in an attempt to "help" them may not work out so well. Think about how your "good words or actions" will be received or perceived by the others you are wanting to give help to. We all have our own life experiences and beliefs which impact our sense of pride and self-worth; think about how to deliver your "good words or actions" so that they do not cause harm to someone else's self-worth.

I have often fallen into the "I know what's best for you" trap. I am pretty sure my wife would tell you that I am somewhat of an expert at it. This is not the behaviour of the person I want to be, so I am learning how to do good things for others in considered and respectful ways. Now when I feel the desire to give or do something for a group or individual, I am reminding myself to take the time to learn about what they really need. I ask myself:

- Am I practising my active listening and questioning skills?
- Am I supporting this person to find their own solutions?
- Am I respecting that this person will need to have their own experiences and make their own mistakes to grow and develop?
- Am I providing help and support with genuine intent of assisting them in ways that are suitable to them?

SURPRISING DISCOVERIES

Know When and How to Say No

If we have a particular skill and attribute and people see us freely giving our time and energy, we will get invitations to give more of our time and energy. This is good when we are looking for opportunities to help others. At some point, we may realise that we are giving more of our time and energy than we are comfortable with and we may start to feel resentment to these people who are inviting us to give.

A good way to manage this is to set clear boundaries. Be clear in your own mind about how much time and energy you will give. I give (time/energy/money) to (people/causes/groups). I will give approximately (hours) per week or month to this (group/action). I am happy to do (describe the activity) for (person/group) and I expect nothing in return.

Here is one of my examples.

For many years, my wife and I performed music at gigs and events, and we also facilitated community drum circles. We were often invited to perform or run drum circles at community events, which we loved to do. Over time our community drum circles became popular and we were invited to give away more of our time and energy. We started to feel uncomfortable with the amount we were giving away so we decided that we needed to be clear about how much time we would give and what type of events we would support.

We set clear boundaries in our own minds regarding which community events and community groups we would support each year. For example, Dragons Abreast is one of the local groups we supported. We also supported the Mental Health and Wellbeing Community Fair, the Reclaim the Night March and the Relay for

Life - cancer fundraiser. That means if they invited us to give our time and energy, we would do whatever we could to be there.

From time to time we may have chosen to support other community events, but we became very comfortable saying no or charging a performance fee. We knew that we were already giving to numerous groups and community events. We would simply thank them for the invitation, let them know that we had already donated our time and skills to numerous groups and events and offer to provide a quote for our services.

A Final Note About Saying and Doing Things That Are Good for Others

It has not come easily or naturally to me, but I have started to learn how to let others say nice things to me and accept it. I have started to more regularly say things like, "Yes, I would like your help, thank you". If you really don't need or want the help that is offered to you, you can thank them and explain why you don't need it at this time. Accepting help from others is good for both you and them. You get the help you need, and they get to reinforce their autopilot regarding the type of person they want to be. It's a win-win. I referred to this earlier when I discussed my HYHM (Help You Help Me) theory.

Talking about my theories…. here is another one. Well it's a law of giving and receiving for me, and it goes like this.

If you give with the genuine intent of it being good for others, you can only ever receive more than you give. Let me say that again. If you give with the genuine intent of it being good for others, you can only ever receive more than you give. I believe this law works when you know in your conscious and unconscious mind that your intention is good.

Here is one of the many examples that have reinforced this law for me in my life.

Years ago, when I was working for the disability employment service, I came to understand that it was not the person's disability that prevented them from gaining and maintaining meaningful employment, it was their beliefs and state of mental wellness. I often tried to connect job seekers with mental health service providers only to discover that the service provider would not work with that person or did not provide the service I had expected them to provide. I spent a while being disillusioned and disgruntled with the local mental health services until finally, I came to the conclusion that I needed to learn more about them so that I could better understand how to assist my clients.

I started to attend the local mental health network meetings and quickly came to understand that my beliefs and expectations were unreasonable. Some services did not take on my clients because they did not actually do what I had wanted them to do, or I was referring my clients to the wrong services, or there was just not a local service that did what I wanted. I also came to understand that even if I did refer to the right service and even if they did take in my client, nothing would really change unless my client decided that they wanted to make the change.

Now I understood that it was difficult for people to find the services they needed and that sometimes the service did not even exist in our region. I decided to support our community to change this. I became actively engaged in the network, and although I had no background in mental health, I was voted to be chair of the network. I knew that I was one of the least educated, least knowledgeable people in the room regarding mental health practices. I also understood that great things can come from well-run meetings and I knew how to run a good meeting. I knew how to make the meetings worthwhile for people to attend and share their knowledge, resources and goodwill. This quickly became a very dynamic network and the outcome for our community was that more people got the service they needed. Network members worked together to provide solutions for local people, we attracted government funding, and our members secured access to mental health support services for local youth.

I knew in my heart and mind that I had accepted the role as chair and devoted a significant amount of my time to the network because I wanted to support the members to do what they did best, which in turn would be good for my community and the people I served in my work.

From that activity, I found a whole new network of friends and business associates. I also learnt a lot about mental health practices, which has benefited me in my personal life and my work. Through this network I was offered a much higher paying job that exposed me to new learning and new networks, and most importantly I got to feel good about myself because I knew that my intention was good.

Personal Vision

Look at any successful business and you will find that they have a Vision Statement. They have taken the time to think about what they want to be. The vision statement is usually not what they are now; it is their future aspirations.

Your personal vision statement describes the person you aspire to be and gives you a direction in life. You use your vision statement

SURPRISING DISCOVERIES

to help you make daily decisions about the things you do and don't do. It helps you focus your time and energy on becoming the person you want to be and living the life you want.

Your personal vision statement is not about material things. It is about the person you want to be, the way you live your life, and it considers how your words and actions impact the lives of others.

It might take a few goes to get your vision statement exactly the way you want it.

You know it is right when you feel connected and inspired by your vision of the future you.

You want your vision statement to stretch you beyond your current reality but still be achievable in the foreseeable future.

If in the next five years you could become the person that you really want to be, what would you be like? What are the types of things you would think about? What would you feel about yourself? What are the types of things you would say? What are the types of things you would do? Are the things you would say and do good for others? Would you feel a sense of fulfilment if you were this person?

For many years we were taught that the human brain becomes pretty set in its ways once we reach adulthood, so you might be thinking that it is too late for you to set a vision statement and make changes in the way you think and act. Scientists now have a much better understanding of brain plasticity and have proven that we can change our neural pathways with sustained practice of new behaviours. So, there are no excuses; it is never too late to set your sights on becoming the person you always wanted to be.

If you are currently unsure what brings fulfilment to your life, do or revise your **Dream Life Interview.**

Tips for writing your personal vision statement
- Write your statement in the present tense, as if you have already become that person
- State your aspirations, passions and purpose
- Think about the things that you value and your talents
- Consider how your personal vision impacts the lives of others
- Ask yourself, "How do I want to spend my life?"
- Write about the person you want to be, not the person you don't want to be.

Things to include
- Your aspiration, passion, purpose
- Your values
- How your vision impacts the lives of others.

Things that do not belong in your personal vision statement
- Financial aspirations
- Material goals (these can be included when you set your goals).

Keep it short and to the point (one or two sentences)
- I am a …..
- To be a …………….. and to be known for……..
- I inspire others to ………..
- I wake each day with the knowledge that I …………
- I spend my time ………..
- I behave like I am ……………..

SURPRISING DISCOVERIES

Four actions to research and plan your good life adventure:

1. **Write your Vision Statement**
   The information above will assist you with this process, and you can research more about it on the internet.

   If you have the **Good Life Game Plan** companion manual, go to the **My Personal Vision** section.

2. **Observe with curiosity how you respond in unfamiliar situations.**

3. **Observe when you are doing things that benefit others, with genuine good intent.**
   How does that make you feel?

4. **If someone offers to do something that is good for you and you think their intent is genuine.** Graciously let them and thank them for their help. It's a win/win.

> "Life is like riding a bicycle. To keep your balance, you must keep moving."
> *Albert Einstein*

PART 5

Finding Affinity

Balance[4]

Noun

1. An even distribution of weight enabling someone or something to remain upright and steady.
2. A situation in which different elements are equal or in the correct proportions.
2.1. Mental or emotional stability.

Verb

1. Put (something) in a steady position so that it does not fall.
2. Offset or compare the value of (one thing) with another.
2.1. Counteract or equal the effect or importance of.
2.2. Establish equal or appropriate proportions of elements in.

How's your balance - are you feeling a sense of affinity with your life?

When we don't find the right balance in our lives, we can feel that sense of tension, disconnection or instability. We might literally feel it in our stomachs; that upset or distressed feeling that we can't quite put our finger on. We might feel it in our neck, shoulders, or back, or our head might ache. We might struggle to get a good night's sleep and wake each morning still feeling exhausted.

If we continue to live an imbalanced life we can become physically ill, and sometimes these illnesses are debilitating and life-threatening.

Have you ever known someone who was ill or injured and their illness or injury got worse because they did not help themselves get better?

Now we will explore what it means to live a balanced life so that you can better understand the things that will bring a greater sense of balance and affinity in your life.

It can be easy for our lives to become imbalanced, in fact, I did it just last year, and it took me months to realise what I was doing to myself. I will share that experience with you but first, you might be thinking, what is this balance you speak of? My life is busy. I don't have the time and energy to do everything. If you are thinking this, you are right. It's not realistic to expect that we are going to be fully focused on all aspects of our life every day. Some parts of our life are going to need to be prioritised over others from time to time. The trick is, recognising that sustaining this imbalance for long periods of time may result in some undesirable consequences.

FINDING AFFINITY

What we are talking about here is finding the right balance for you, the right balance for your life. The tools I am sharing with you will help you decide what that balance will be.

Here Is One of My Many Life Out of Balance Stories

Our company was contracted to do work for another company. We had been in this contract for a number of years and I was very aware of the high financial and reputational risk associated with this work, so as the CEO I regularly monitored our performance.

We previously had a very good team working on this contract, but due to relocation and career changes, we had lost a number of key team members. I had moved one of our most experienced staff back into that contract and we set about recruiting and training new team members. It took us a number of attempts and nearly 12 months to put the right team together. There was a backlog of work and I could see that the team leader was overwhelmed so I had started to actively work on that contract as well as trying to keep up with my CEO duties. For a couple of months, the team leader and I regularly worked six to seven days a week, with some days being 12 to 14 hours long. No matter how much time we threw at it we could not get on top of it; there were just so many problems. One Friday night I was at home eating an unhealthy dinner, feeling at my wit's end and planning for another weekend at work. I did not know what to do so I turned to my life planning app (this is a list of questions I sometimes ask myself about my sense of balance in life and what I would like to be different).

Here is how I answered the question "What would I like to change?".

I would like to feel better. Currently have regular earache, and jaw, neck and shoulders ache. Fuzzy head. Lower back and hips so tight and sore is restricting my movement. Pain when I sit, stand or even walk. Tense muscles in my stomach - feel sick. Throat restricted. Blurry in my right eye. Feelings of hopelessness. Lay awake for hours in the night. Tired in the mornings. Struggle to focus on tasks. Thoughts of trapped and escaping. The dread of failing. Not able to relax when not working. Working longer hours but not feeling productive. Can't find a solution to fix outstanding contract compliance. Guilty for not finding solutions earlier in the year. Overwhelmed. Crying or feeling like crying most days. Not good enough. Past my prime - limited future options. Risk of losing my home. Don't want to socialise. No joy, lack of interest in things I usually enjoy. Loss of passion or care about helping angry, unreasonable clients.

I read back through what I had written and was shocked. These are all clear signs of burnout and that means I am not thinking clearly, I am not thinking creatively, I am not thinking with a solution mindset. I am doing exactly the opposite of what I would coach people to do in this situation.

I jumped online and immediately booked the weekend in a rainforest cabin. We drove up there the next day and spent the afternoon having a light walk in the rainforest. I did not feel relaxed because I was worried about the problems back at work, but I decided to trust in the process. We went to the resort restaurant for dinner and had an early night. To my surprise, I slept well and woke early the next morning. I did not want to disturb my wife, so I went for a walk. I walked for a while until finally, I started to notice my surroundings. I was by a river in a beautiful rainforest. I sat down on the riverbank and watched the birds and the platypus go about their daily life. For the first time in months, I noticed something good in life and I felt better. Over the next few months, I spent many of my weekends camping in lovely places with my wife. I felt so much better, my thinking was clearer, I found solutions and we met the deadline.

In a balanced life, we are regularly spending time and energy on all the parts of our lives, including the ones that bring us health, joy and fulfilment. We are investing ourselves in our family and friends, our social activities, our career, our finances, our physical and mental health and our spirituality.

In acknowledging that we will often find ourselves out of balance, we can do things to help us notice when this is happening and make adjustments to our life so that we don't become completely lopsided and topple over.

Two actions to research and plan your good life adventure:

1. Download your Free copy of the **Wheel of Life** from www.thevillageleaders.com.au
   The **Wheel of Life** will assist you to better understand your balance in relation to your family and friends, relationships, social activities, career, finances, physical and mental health, spirituality, personal development, creativity and play.

   If you have the **Good Life Game Plan** companion manual, review the **Balancing Act** section and complete the **Wheel of Life**.

2. Download and have a test run at completing the questions in the **Life Planning App**.

   Earlier, I mentioned my **Life Planning App** and an online questionnaire that I have designed for myself. You can download the free Google or Microsoft Forms Template.

   Once you download and duplicate the Wheel of Life and Life Planning App forms in your own accounts, the information you enter is not shared with me, it stays in your account.

   I have also included a list of the questions I ask myself in the appendices of this book.

"It is difficult to say what is impossible, for the dream of yesterday is the hope of today and the reality of tomorrow."

Robert H. Goddard

PART 6

To Infinity and Beyond

Reality[4]
Noun
1. The state of things as they actually exist, as opposed to an idealistic or notional idea of them.
1.1. A thing that is actually experienced or seen, especially when this is unpleasant.
1.2. A thing that exists in fact, having previously only existed in one's mind.
2. The state or quality of having existence or substance.
2.1. Existence that is absolute, self-sufficient, or objective, and not subject to human decisions or conventions.

In Part 5, I talked about one of the tools I use to better understand my current reality. I know that understanding and accepting my current reality will help me to envisage and create my preferred reality.

Sometimes it can be very tempting to fall into a cycle of thinking that life is unfair and has singled us out. We notice all the things going wrong in our lives and we start complaining and blaming. Some people spend their entire life stuck in the "life is unfair", complaining, blaming mindset. You will know people stuck in this mindset because they will regularly talk about all the things they don't like about their life and they do nothing about changing it.

We can all identify the things we don't like in our life. In fact, many of us think about it and talk about it often. We can get stuck in a loop of thinking about it over and over and over for days, weeks, months and even years. It is exactly this type of thinking that keeps us trapped in a life we don't want for ourselves. We can even get stuck in relationships or activities that are really harmful to us.

If we don't clearly understand and accept our current reality, our current thinking, our current words, our current actions, we won't be able to move to a more preferred reality.

I am very aware that, like everyone else, I can be vulnerable to falling into this thinking trap. While it is easy to identify when other people are doing it, it can be very tricky to know when I am doing it to myself. That is why I regularly use tools to support me to identify my current reality and know what I am thinking, saying and doing about it.

I know that if I continue to focus on the things I don't want, I will not get the things I do want. I know that if I want my life to be different, I need to think differently.

We are now going to discuss the concepts of current reality and preferred reality in more detail so that you understand the barriers to achieving your preferred reality and know what you can do to help overcome these barriers. We will also discuss some tools to help you define your current and preferred reality.

Current Reality to Preferred Reality

Our current reality is how we experience our life now.
Our preferred reality is how we would prefer to experience our life.
Once we have clearly defined our preferred reality, we can make a plan to move from our current reality to our preferred reality.

For example, my Current Health Reality was like this:

- I overeat, resulting in being over my preferred weight with increased health risks.
- My hips, knees, ankles and heels are often sore, and I regularly feel uncomfortable, and my heart beats harder after I eat.
- I currently wear size 18 clothes.
- I eat breakfast at about 6.30 am (cereal or toast).
- I often feel hungry and eat again at about 9.30 am.
- I eat lunch at about 12.30 pm (this is often bought from the café, and a large meal). I often want something sweet straight after lunch and I feel sleepy after lunch.

- I get a sweet craving at about 3.00 pm and eat biscuits, cake, lollies or chocolate.
- I eat dinner between 7.30 pm and 8.30 pm. Sometimes I just have alcohol and an unhealthy snack.
- I often don't feel like preparing my meals.
- I feel tired and uninspired, so I just sit on the couch and watch unsatisfying TV for a few hours before I go to bed between 10.00pm and 11.00pm.

I defined My Preferred Reality:

- I eat food to sustain a healthy mind and body.
- My body feels good, and I feel comfortable after I eat.
- I comfortably wear size 12 to 14 clothes.
- I drink about four glasses of water between when I wake and 8.30 am.
- I eat my breakfast between 8.30 am and 9.30 am (egg and veg or chia pudding and fruit or couscous, yoghurt and fruit or quinoa yoghurt and fruit.)
- I drink water between breakfast and lunch. I can have limited amounts of black tea (I like black tea).
- I eat lunch between 12.30pm and 1.30pm. I have prepared my own healthy meal.
- If I crave an afternoon snack, I first drink a couple of glasses of water. I check if I am actually feeling hungry or just habitually craving food because my autopilot is programmed to eat sugary food when I am feeling tired or distressed.
- If I am genuinely hungry (be honest with myself) I eat a healthy snack that I have on hand for such an occasion.
- I do an activity before and after work like swim, garden, take the dogs for a walk on the beach, washing, cleaning or healthy food prep.

- I eat dinner between 6.30 pm and 7.30 pm.
- I read a book, study or do something creative. Sometimes I relax in front of the television.
- I go to bed between 9.00 pm and 10.00 pm.

My 10-Step Plan to Move from My Current Reality to My Preferred Reality

Step 1   Describe what I want and when I want it (set a realistic and achievable date) and why I want it (why is this important to me).

Step 2   Describe it as if I have already achieved it. What does it look, sound, smell and taste like?

Step 3   Describe how I feel about achieving it.

Step 4   Write down who helped me complete it.

Step 5   Write the list of actions I took to achieve it.

Step 6   Write my preferred reality scripts about it. (I turn these into one of my Life Songs).

Step 7   Write myself a letter so that in the coming weeks, I can consciously use it as my map when my autopilot tries to steer me back onto the old programmed path.

Step 8   Check my commitment to this change. Is this in my current top three priorities?

Step 9   Do the actions; consciously say my preferred reality scripts or sing my song.

Step 10   Observe myself with curiosity and respect, notice when my autopilot has slipped me back to old habits and consciously steer myself to my new habits. Just keep doing it and trust that change will come with repetitive action.

It's that easy right! Just decide what you want in your life, make a plan and follow the plan.

It is that easy ….. there's just that little matter of being a human with an unconscious mind that naturally resists change.

I talk a lot about how our automatic pilot or unconscious mind works to keep us on track because it has such a significant impact on our life. It sticks with the program, and it repeatedly and automatically does the things that it knows how to do. We are very lucky to have such an amazingly powerful mind working for us; it just means we need to put in some time and conscious effort to reprogram our habits to match our preferred reality.

You will know many people who will refuse to even consider that they can reprogram their mind and change their life. They will regularly complain about their current reality and will be very skilled at making excuses as to why their life cannot change. They will be experts at blaming others, and they will resist taking responsibility for their own thoughts, feelings, words and actions.

You will also know people who decided that they did want to make changes in their life, but they gave up and failed to make the changes they wanted for themselves. These people will also start making convincing excuses; they will blame themselves or others for the failure. They may also fall into the trap of not taking responsibility for their own thoughts, feelings, words and actions.

This is often referred to as Resistance To Change and it is a normal and natural human behaviour. If you take notice of the people around you, you will start seeing just how much this resistance to change is keeping people stuck in a life they don't want for themselves.

I have seen it over and over again in my work and my social networks. I have spent the past 25 years working for organisations that have the core purpose of helping people. Helping people get a job so they can afford to put a roof over their head and feed themselves or have more life choices and feel a sense of purpose. Helping people find support with their mental health needs, helping people connect with and engage in their community, helping people have somewhere to live, a safe place they can call home. Through these experiences, I came to understand that it does not matter what you give to people, it does not matter what you do for people, it does not matter what you say to people. Their life will not improve unless they decide that they want to change, unless they make the decision to do something about it, unless they actually do what they said they were going to do, unless they consciously and persistently override their autopilot, unless they take responsibility for themselves. When I say they I mean we - we all experience resistance to change but it is only resistance and we can consciously push back. We can decide what changes we want to make, we can make a plan, we can take action and we can stick to it.

When I was working at the employment service, some of my clients asked me to assist them because they were being financially or emotionally abused in their home environment. While I could not go into the home and stop that behaviour, I could offer to connect my clients with services that may be able to assist them, and we could support them to find another place to live.

My colleagues and I understood that the person moving out of the abusive home was not necessarily going to be a long term change. We had seen on numerous occasions, a person would decide to move into their own place and reduce or completely stop all contact with the perpetrator. The person first reported they were very happy with this change and that they had started a new life with a job and their own place to live. After a period of time, they would reconnect with the perpetrator. Then there would be some event that led them to decide to move back in with the perpetrator. They ended up living back in the environment they had so desperately wanted to escape and now they had a belief that they could not make it out on their own. What they did not understand was that their desire to go back to the old place was just their autopilot sticking to the program; if they had stuck to the change their autopilot would have eventually been reprogrammed and their life would have improved.

If you want a more visual understanding about our response to change, the J Curve is a great example. You can research the J Curve on the internet.

Our resistance to change or our autopilot is not judgemental, it just sticks to the program, whatever that program is. How many times have you heard of a rich person whose business went belly up and they lost everything only to see that one or two years later they had another business and were living the high life again?

I will never forget one woman I had the privilege of working with who had acquired a brain injury through a motor vehicle accident. It was a life-threatening accident. She was unconscious and the doctors had informed her family that she would most likely not survive once they turned the life support systems off. They said that even if she did survive, her brain damage was so severe that she would not be able to walk, talk, feed herself or have any quality of life. The family finally came to the heartbreaking decision that the best thing to do for her was to turn the machines off. This turned out to be the best thing because she was quite a determined woman. When they turned the machines off, she woke up and the doctors were proven correct - she could not walk, she could not talk, she could not feed herself. What the doctors did not know was that her unconscious mind understood what a determined person she was, and it stuck to the program. She learnt to talk, she learnt to walk, and she learnt to feed herself. By the time I met her, she had developed her systems to manage her brain injury and she was ready to return to work. She was no longer licenced in her previous profession because it was considered the brain injury had impacted her ability to do that work.

I spent time learning about her and observed how committed she was to improve her current situation and that she would do whatever was in her power to do.

We agreed that while she could not work in her previous profession, she could still work in that industry, so I set about contacting employers on her behalf. We found an employer and she started working, she also did much more than that. She commenced re-studying her previous profession and her employer offered her the opportunity to use her skills. Over time she finished her studies and she again became fully qualified in her preferred profession.

I believe her autopilot kicked in and worked until she was back on track. It did not intentionally make her life better or worse, it just followed the program.

We previously discussed that we can choose our own thoughts and learn to regularly ask ourselves, "What Am I Thinking?". We now know that we can imagine our preferred reality and make a plan to move to that preferred reality. We also know that we have a powerful mind working for us that we can reprogram.

Albert Einstein's famous quote is relevant here:

> **"Imagination is everything. It is the preview of life's coming attractions."**

When we see our preferred reality in our own mind's eye, when we hear it in our internal conversations, when we feel it in our heart, when we consciously and consistently take action, our unconscious mind starts to learn a new program and it begins to support us in making the changes we want in our life.

Tools We Can Use to Change Our Mind

Preferred Reality Scripts

We each have things that we say to ourselves over and over and over again. These are a set of scripts that cycle through our mind, and we often don't even know what we are saying to ourselves. That is why it is important to regularly ask ourselves questions like, "What Am I Thinking? Do these thoughts match my preferred reality? Are these thoughts good for me?".

When we are thinking thoughts that keep us stuck in the life we don't want for ourselves, we can use our readily prepared set of Preferred Reality Scripts to consciously replace the unwanted thoughts. A well-written and practised set of Preferred Reality Scripts is the description of our future life. I turn my Preferred Reality Scripts into my **Life Songs** because it makes it much easier for me to remember them, I enjoy singing them and I get to pick the music I put them to. I often catch myself unconsciously singing one of my **Life Songs** and I know that the words in the song match my preferred life. We will learn more about our preferred reality scripts in Part 8 of this book.

Visualisation and Images
Our brain learns from the things that it regularly sees, so you can use visualisations and look at images to help reprogram your mind. You can do this through mindfulness, meditation and vision boards. We will discuss this further later in this book, and there are plenty of resources available online to learn about visualisation and vision boards. You can attend meditation classes and there are many apps and books that will support you with your mindfulness, meditations and vision boards.

Mindfulness and Meditation
When I learnt how to become a mindset coach, I was introduced to the concept of using Largo Baroque music to achieve an alpha mind state. There are some studies that linked the alpha mind state with increased creativity, feeling calmer and improved memory. Some of these studies have been challenged in more recent times[5]. Nonetheless, I found the practice of mindfulness and meditation very useful over many years. There are lots of different mindfulness and meditation options available to you and I have listed some of my favourites on the next page.

Spiritual Meditation

I first learned about spiritual meditation in my early 20's when I was discovering lots of new wonders in life. I was starting to understand that there were so many more possibilities than had been revealed to me in my youth. I engaged in many spiritual and personal development activities. I became a massage therapist, learned about guided breathing techniques, Reiki, aromatherapy and meditation. My then-partner and I set up our small business and immersed ourselves in the world of spirituality and natural therapy. At that time in my life, I was still stuck in the belief that I would always be alone, so my autopilot assisted me to say and do things to deliver on that belief; hence our relationship did not last.

When we separated, she kept the business and went on to become a successful health and wellbeing business owner, author and speaker. I discovered my love for working in the community sector. Thirty years later I am still so very grateful for the time we shared and the things we learnt together. It seems like many lifetimes ago, but my long-term health and wellbeing has benefited from learning about aromatherapy and spiritual meditation. Over the years I have used guided meditation recordings and attended meditation groups. I don't always use spiritual meditations but there are times when I do want to feel more spiritually connected to myself and others.

Non-Spiritual Meditation

Meditation does not need to be attached to any spiritual beliefs or practices.

Just the act of spending a few minutes focusing on our breathing is meditation and helps our mind to see alternative options in our life. There are plenty of free meditation apps available, and one of my favourites is "Let's Meditate" by Heal Me Team. Other popular apps are "Smiling Mind," "Headspace for Meditation, Mindfulness and Sleep," and "Calm - Meditate, Sleep, Relax".

Why not download an app today and give it a go? If you already use a meditation app, you are welcome to post it on the **Beyond Possible** Facebook group and share why you like this app.

There are so many other meditation options, and it is worth the effort to find the ones that work for you. Sometimes I have had phases in my life where I can't seem to just sit still and breathe so I have done Djembe Drumming or Shamanic drumming meditations. Other options include walking meditations, yoga meditations, singing bowl meditations, and chanting meditations. If you are not ready for meditation you can do anything that helps you find your state of flow, that state where you fully immerse yourself in an activity and lose all track of time as you are completely focused on that thing.

Combining Meditation and Visualisation
One of the techniques I learnt was to sit and listen to Largo Baroque music and visualise the changes I wanted in my life. Largo Baroque music is believed to support concentration, and if you do an online search you will find playlists available on YouTube and other streaming services.

I have enjoyed some profound experiences when I practice sitting meditatively while listening to Largo Baroque music and visualising a preferred reality. A few years ago, our team was managing a particularly complex contract. Each team member was displaying signs of distress and some were not performing at the level required to fulfil our contractual obligations. I was also feeling distressed and lying awake at night for hours, engaging in thoughts of blame and escapism. On this particular night I made up my mind that

I had had enough, I was going to the Board of Directors the very next day to tell them that it was me or the contract. If they wanted to keep that contract they would need to find a new CEO. The next morning, I woke still feeling very distressed and in desperation, I put on my headphones and played Largo Baroque music. At first, I just let the music calm me and bring a sense of joy. I then started to imagine walking into work and seeing a team of happy and productive staff. I thought about each individual staff member and I wished them well.

I got ready and went to work. I walked into the office and saw each one of these people who I had just sent well wishes to and I knew that we could not give up that contract because most of these people would lose their job. This meditation was profound for me because it helped me to change my thinking from a blaming and escapism mentality to being solution-focused with an "I can do this" mentality. I negotiated with our contract partner, I worked with the team to re-define our systems and processes and I negotiated with the board to increase our wage budget so that I could recruit more staff to help clear the backlog of work. In a short time, the stress levels started to reduce, the team was happier, and I had not taken the self-harming action of delivering an unreasonable ultimatum to the board.

Kindness
It is very important that we speak to ourselves in a positive, supportive and non-judgemental way. If we get stuck in blame and negative thoughts patterns our unconscious mind will continue to act in accordance with this negative self-programming.

If we learn how to observe ourselves with curiosity, we can start to notice our thoughts, feelings, words and actions. We can accept that these are our current programmed responses and be grateful for noticing them. We can then practice our preferred reality scripts, visualisations and images. We can remain calm and find creative solutions, and we can keep doing the actions to reprogram our unconscious mind and move to our preferred reality. I found the book, "The Kindness Method: Changing Habits for Good" by Shahroo Izadi very helpful in understanding how I could introduce more self-kindness into my life. The book is on my recommended reading list.

In my work example above, I had moved into a blaming mentality and it is often very tempting for us to blame others or external forces for the way our life currently is. We might blame someone from our childhood, someone that we have or had a relationship with, someone or something at work, a natural disaster, the government, the church, etc. The truth is, blaming others and external forces is a complete cop-out. Engaging in blame is a way of letting ourselves off the hook for not taking responsibility for our own thoughts, feelings, words and actions. Yes, there are things that happen in our lives that are out of our control and sometimes these things are petty in the scheme of life, but we dwell on them, and sometimes they are pretty grim, and sometimes they are life-changing. These are our obstacles in life, and we all have them. None of us gets a smooth, easy ride through our entire life. Some of us see the obstacles as burdensome problems and some of us see them as challenges to be met and the opportunity for growth. Imagine how boring your life would be if you were never challenged or had the opportunity to grow and learn. Think about the things that have been hard in your life and that sense of satisfaction when you moved through that challenge.

I now know that I can't control everything that happens in my life, but I can change how I react to these things. Sometimes I still catch myself engaging in blame and escapism; at these times I am thinking, saying and doing things that don't match my personal vision. Rather than blaming myself for this, I thank myself for noticing and ask myself What Am I Thinking **(W.A.I.T?)**, I do meditations and other mindfulness activities to help me move back into a solutions and opportunities mindset. We can consciously decide our own thoughts, which will influence our feelings, words and actions. This is called resilience and it improves our quality of life.

Changing your thinking may seem hard or even impossible. It does take commitment and it is absolutely possible. You don't need to change everything at once, in fact, it is much better to start making little changes. Remember to **W.A.I.T?** often so that you start to learn more about your current thinking and belief patterns. By continuing to read this book you are learning the tools and tips to manage your resistance to change and create your good life.

TO INFINITY AND BEYOND

Actions to define your preferred reality:

Work through the Current Reality and Preferred Reality questions in the appendices of this book under these headings:

- **Current Reality,**
- **Preferred Reality,**
- **How I Spend my Time,**
- **My Health,**
- **Learn and Grow,**
- **Finances.**

If you have the **Good Life Game Plan** companion manual, you will find all the activities in the **Current Reality to Preferred Reality** section.

When we change our mind, we change our life. Invest time in yourself; your future self will be grateful that you did.

"Rowing harder doesn't help if the boat is headed in the wrong direction."

Kenichi Ohmae

PART 7

Forecasting the Future

Program[4]

Noun

1. A set of related measures or activities with a particular long-term aim.
1.1. A planned series of future events or performances.
2. A series of coded software instructions to control the operation of a computer or other machine.

Verb

1. Provide (a computer or other machine) with coded instructions for the automatic performance of a task.
1.1. *no object* Write computer programs.

1.2. Input (instructions for the automatic performance of a task) into a computer or other machine.
1.3. Cause (a person or animal) to behave in a predetermined way.
2. Arrange according to a plan or schedule.
2.1. Schedule (an item) within a plan.

What are the differences between dreams and goals?
Have you ever set goals and achieved them?
Have you ever set goals and not achieved them?
Are you feeling really excited about the prospect of setting some goals or are you dreading it? Are you tempted to put this book down and never read it again?

Either way…. I've got your back.

To you who are excited, have a quick read through these next paragraphs and move on.

To you who are dreading it. Firstly, I want you to know that it's ok, plenty of people don't want to do goal setting and even people who do enjoy doing goal setting often don't get it quite right, including me. We can always learn more about our goals.

If you are really going to put this book down, please don't throw it away. Recognise that this response is coming from your autopilot and over the coming days, weeks, months or even years you might consciously decide that you want to change your life. You might decide to override your autopilot. If you keep this book somewhere safe, it will be there, waiting for you when you are ready. In the meantime, be as kind to yourself as you can.

FORECASTING THE FUTURE

If you are deciding to override your autopilot today… let's do this!

For some people, the idea of goal setting seems like a very formal and rigid process, but I believe the best goal setting process is creative and flexible, so I like to call it **My Good Life Game Plan**. It's about being open to possibilities, being creative, being flexible and creating a plan that inspires you. A plan that you believe in, a plan that can change and grow as you learn more about yourself, and a plan that helps you stay on track.

I spent 15 years working in an organisation that assisted people to find a job. I genuinely wanted to help each individual person to develop the career path that suited them. I would invest time to get to know and build a relationship with each person. Then I would start steering the conversation to questions like; "Are there things that you have dreamt about doing or learning?" "Do you have a dream job in mind?". The majority of people said they had no idea and even if they had dreamed about it, they could not express their dreams. Through their past life experiences, they were limiting their own thinking about the possibilities in their life. On the other end of the spectrum I sometimes met people who did have dreams, in fact, they had grand dreams that were not based in any level of reality.

So how can we know our dreams and then decide which of these dreams can be turned into achievable goals?

First, we need to allow ourselves to dream. If we don't know our dreams we limit our possibilities, and we may even start to believe that our life is pretty boring. For those of us who do know our dreams, we need to make plans and take action. We don't want to end up living in a dream world that never becomes our real life.

I have met plenty of people who have what I call the "I'm Gonna" Syndrome. You will know people who say they are going to do things, but they never actually get around to finishing it, often they never even start it, they are just stuck in "I'm Gonna" dream land.

Now that we know how to think about our current reality and our preferred reality, we need to make sure we are accepting our current reality so that we can make an effective plan to move to our preferred reality. If we don't acknowledge and accept our current reality we may have thoughts like, life is not fair, I can never get what I want, someone or something is to blame. Continuing with these types of thoughts can lead to feelings of disgruntlement, distress, jealousy or depression and stop us from moving forward with the words and actions needed to create our preferred reality.

Now you will learn more about turning your dreams into your **Good Life Game Plan**.

You will understand how to decide which dreams you want to become a reality. You will learn about short, medium and long term goals, and I will give you the tools to get started on your plans.

As a young adult, I had impossible dreams…I dreamed of becoming a manager/leader, I dreamed of buying my own home, I dreamed of doing something worthwhile with my life, and I dreamed of finding love. All of these dreams became my reality, so I dreamed even more impossible dreams….I dreamed of having enough money, I dreamed of becoming a musician, I dreamed of buying a different home, I dreamed of having enough time, I dreamed of being even more open to love, I dreamed of getting married, I dreamed of having friends to spend my time with and I dreamed of feeling safe in the world. All these dreams became my reality.

FORECASTING THE FUTURE

Dreams vs Fantasies

Dreams are a great starting point when we are thinking about what would make a good life. Not all of our dreams will turn out to be good for us. Sometimes they are about avoidance or escapism, and if we really did what we dreamt about doing we would end up feeling very unfulfilled or worse.

How many times have you heard someone say that their dream is to go and live on a desert island so they can get away from their busy and stressful life?

A desert island is usually uninhabited by other humans because it is not a good place for humans to live. There might be limited or no drinkable water and food supply. It might be prone to extreme weather, and it would soon become a very lonely place to be. So, when a person says they want to live on a desert island are they saying that they want to suffer and die, and they want to be alone in the process of dying? Most people don't really want this experience; what they really want is a way to relieve the day to day pressures they are feeling in their current life. I am reminded here of the wisdom in being careful about what we wish for.

The dream of living on a desert island is really a fantasy based on escapism. You will know people (whether they tell you or not) who have fantasies about ending their own life. They may have particular dying scenarios they play out in their mind, but it is quite likely they don't really want the end result of being dead. They just want some of the things they are regularly thinking and feeling to stop.

If you are having suicidal thoughts, please know that the world is better off with you and you can get help. There is a lot of support out there, so please ask for help from someone you trust or contact any of these support services; Lifeline on 131114, Suicide Call Back Service on 1300 659 467 or have a look at the resources and contacts at Beyond Blue - beyondblue.org.au. If you are at immediate risk call 000 or visit your nearest hospital.

Some people dream about acquiring particular material possessions or a level of power or a title because they believe this will make them feel better about themselves and their life. At the end of the day, all that stuff and things is just stuff and things. If we, in ourselves, have not changed, we will still be thinking and feeling the same stuff we wanted to escape.

Our useful dreams are the ones that challenge us to become the person we want to be, the person that thinks, says and does the things that we admire and respect. The person who can accept their current reality and imagine their preferred reality, and the person who accepts responsibility for their own thoughts, feelings, words and actions.

FORECASTING THE FUTURE

Let the Game Plan Begin

Filter your Dreams and create your **Good Life Game Plan**.

Before we proceed, go back and do a quick review of everything you have done so far. This information will be very useful in these next activities.
- My Good Life/Dream Year
- Letter to Me
- My Dream Life Interview
- My Personal Vision
- Balancing Act - The Wheel of Life
- Current Reality to Preferred Reality

Work through each of the following activities. These activities are also contained in the **Good Life Game Plan** companion manual with space to record your answers.

Dreams to Reality
Write down which of your dreams are short-term (in the next 12 months), medium-term (1 to 5 years) and long-term (over 5 years).

Goal Filter
Have another look at your short, medium and long term goals and ask yourself these questions for each goal:

What would be the real outcomes of actioning this goal?
Are these outcomes good for me?
Is it morally right and fair for everyone?
Will it challenge me to change the way I think, feel, speak and act?
Will I have the opportunity to learn and grow?
Does it match my personal vision?
Is it realistic and achievable?
Will I make this one of my top three priorities now or in the future?

Top Three - 90 Day Game Plan
Pick one to three of your goals that you want to get started on now.
Describe your goal.
Why do you want it? What date would I like to have achieved it?
What will you do with it?
What does it look, sound, smell, taste like?
Describe your goal as if you have already achieved it.
Who helped you to complete it?
What daily actions did you take to achieve this goal?
Ask yourself: Am I committed to this goal? Will I take the actions to fulfil it?

FORECASTING THE FUTURE

Once you have done these activities, congratulate yourself for completing the goal-setting process.

Give yourself permission to come back and review and tweak them until they are exactly the way you want them to be.

Focus on your 90-day Game Plan. Make the daily actions your top priority and you will start seeing change.

Next, you will learn about the tools that will support you to follow through with your actions.

"Positive thinking will let you do everything better than negative thinking will."

Zig Ziglar

PART 8
The Adventure Seeker Essentials

Mindset[4]
Noun
The established set of attitudes held by someone.

Stickability[4]
Noun
A person's ability to persevere with something; staying power.

I have already discussed how our unconscious mind sticks to the program. Our mind is extremely effective at keeping us on the known path. Through conscious decisions and persistent actions, we can reprogram our unconscious habits. We just need to spend some time noticing the thoughts, words and actions that no longer serve us and consciously practice the thoughts, words and actions that do serve us. We need to notice when our thinking has turned us back towards the old path and understand that this is normal. We can then consciously take actions to steer ourselves to the life we want.

How do you develop your stickability?

Many people say they are going to do this or that thing that is really important to them. They start doing it with a high level of energy and enthusiasm and then they give up; they never make the changes they said they wanted in their life. They make convincing excuses, they engage in blame and they remain stuck in the life they are less than satisfied with. Even if they have set the goals that are right for them and made great action plans that they are committed to, they find themselves slipping back into old habits or just not taking the actions they set for themselves. This is because our unconscious mind does not recognise these new actions as something that we do. It does not see these actions as being a part of who we are, so it works to get us back on track and efficiently operate our day to day life.

Once having tried and failed, people can fall into the trap of believing it impossible for them to make changes in their life. It is not always easy, but it is absolutely possible. It is worth the time and energy we invest in ourselves. When we persistently invest time and energy in ourselves we start to see a positive impact on our own lives, and we can have more positive impacts on the people around us.

Human beings are extremely talented at developing and using tools to make hard things easy and impossible things possible:

THE ADVENTURE SEEKER ESSENTIALS

Humans don't have wings, yet we can fly.
Humans can't breathe underwater, yet we can go to the bottom of the ocean.
Humans have a maximum running speed of 45km per hour, yet we can easily travel 100kms per hour.

What tools do you already use in your everyday life to make hard things easier and impossible things possible?
Will you invest your time and energy to learn which mind-changing tools work best for you? Will you back yourself and keep going even when you are tempted to just slip back into old habits?

Some of you will take the information in this book and run with it, some will reach out for support to learn more about changing your mindset, some of you will start and give up, and some of you will do nothing. I have done all of these things at different stages of my life, and I wish you the best whatever you decide to do or not do. Just know that there are lots of different tools and people out there that can support you with your mindset.

You have learnt how to develop your **Good Life Game Plan,** and now we will focus on developing your preferred reality scripts to support you with achieving your goals.

If you have not completed your Game Plan, I encourage you to do it now as you do need your clearly defined goals and actions to create your preferred reality scripts.

On with The Adventure

Firstly, let's have a think about our language. How can we turn impossible statements into possible statements?

One of the most popular impossible statements that people use is "I can't".

I can't wake in my own bed and then attend a 10.00 am meeting in a city over 1000kms away from my home.
I can't lift heavy things to move them.
I can't write a book.
I can't change my life.

These types of statements keep us stuck in an impossible mindset. It is very important to catch ourselves when we think or say these types of statements so that we can take a moment to define the challenge and think about the opportunity. When we define the challenge and the opportunity we can then come up with our Possible Statement.

Impossible Statement: I can't wake in my own bed and then attend a 10.00 am meeting in a city over 1000kms away from my home.
Challenge and Opportunity Statement: I can't wake in my own bed and then attend a 10.00 am meeting in a city over 1000kms away from my home, but if I catch an early flight or attend via the internet I can.
Possible Statement: I can wake in my own bed and then attend a 10.00 am meeting in a city over 1000kms away from my home by catching an early flight or attending via the internet.

Impossible Statement: I can't lift heavy things to move them.
Challenge and Opportunity Statement: I can't lift heavy things, but if I use my furniture trolly I can.

Possible Statement: I can use my furniture trolly to lift and move heavy things.

Impossible Statement: I can't write a book.
Challenge and Opportunity Statement: I can't write a book, but if I engage an expert I can learn how to.
Possible Statement: I can engage an expert to help me learn how to write a book.

Impossible Statement: I can't change my life.
Challenge and Opportunity Statement: I can't change my life, but if I learn how to use the tools and knowledge that is available to me I can use those tools to create the life I want for myself.
Possible Statement: I can use the tools and knowledge that is available to me to create the life I want for myself.

Go back and re-read the Impossible Statements….how do they make you feel?
Then read the Possible Statements…..how do they make you feel?

Preferred Reality Scripts

Our preferred reality scripts are written to match our personal vision, and our goals. We use them to override and eventually rewrite our program so that when we are operating in autopilot our thoughts, feelings, words and actions match our preferred reality. The trick is writing your preferred reality scripts in a way that really works for you.

I spent years writing out affirmations like "I am slim, fit, healthy and happy". The thing about that statement is I took no responsibility for it. I just kind of thought if I wrote and said it enough I would become slim, fit, healthy and happy or at least I wanted to believe that was all I needed to do. The reality is we don't become slim, fit, healthy and happy unless we take action.

From time to time I achieved my weight goal and I would sustain a good level of activity for 3 to 9 months, but it always felt temporary and I would lapse back into old habits resulting in me returning to being 15kg to 20kg above my desired weight. I would stop doing the movement I had been enjoying and my body aches would return. It took me many years to work out what was going on and I am now very aware that I could lapse if I don't check in with myself regularly.

I believed and still believe that affirmations are a great way to put our goals and intent out into the universe. The act of writing down what we want and sending this message out can often result in external forces presenting the right opportunities to us. Buying my first house was a perfect example of that. I focused my attention and actions on preparing to buy a house, and my boss loaned me the deposit, resulting in me achieving that highly-coveted life-changing goal much quicker than was originally possible.

For my health goals, I behaved like I only needed to state my goal, develop my affirmations and send them out into the universe and voila my desires would be fulfilled with no effort from me.

The fact is, there needed to be actions like putting less food in my body - particularly those sugary and fatty foods - reduce the amount of high sugar and alcoholic drinks and increase my daily amount of fresh fruit and vegetables. Plus add some more movement into my days.

I had even tricked myself into thinking I could outsource the responsibility of buying and preparing my healthy food – like this yummy, healthy food was just going to magically appear when I needed to eat.

So, unless someone kidnapped me, locked me in a room and only provided me with a limited amount of healthy food and then forced me to exercise each day, my affirmations with no plan and no actions were not really helping me become a healthier person. When I finally accepted that I had to do it for myself and that I wanted to do it for myself, everything changed. First, I wrote my goal and a set of preferred reality scripts. This is personal, but I think it is important that I share it with you.

My Goal: To be healthy and feel comfortable in my body. This means being able to comfortably fit into size 12 to 14 clothes, walk, bend, bounce, twist, lift, stretch and balance. I am strong enough to easily do day to day tasks. I can climb on ladders, ride a bike, swim, dance, and play games. I also have good stamina, a healthy heart, good lung capacity, and can sustain physical activity.

My Preferred Reality Scripts:
Today I am looking after my body.
I buy foods that are good for me like fruit, vegetables and legumes.
I make the time to prepare healthy meals.
I am aware of my body and I only eat what I need.
I eat slowly and pay attention to the food and drinks I am choosing to put in my body.
I move my body every day.

These preferred reality scripts remind me that I am taking ownership of my actions. They also give much clearer instructions to my unconscious mind compared to my previous affirmations.

I was amazed by the things that happened once I started regularly saying my preferred reality scripts and following my Game Plan for this goal.

My cravings for sugary foods and chips reduced significantly and it became much easier for me to manage my food intake. I also came to the understanding that I was not going to die of starvation if I did not feel stuffed with food most of the day. I become very comfortable with not constantly putting food in my mouth, in fact, I much preferred to give my stomach time between meals rather than that uncomfortable overfull feeling. My wife saw the types of foods I was now wanting to eat and adjusted what she bought when it was her turn to do the grocery shopping (ok she mostly does the grocery shopping). The weight started to fall off me, and I felt better. I do still catch myself falling back into old comfort eating habits sometimes and I thank myself for noticing. I would often realise that I had not used my preferred health reality scripts for a while and would practice my scripts, which supported me to get back on my desired track.

Tips for Writing Your Preferred Reality Scripts

1. Make sure they complement your personal vision, your goals and your game plan
2. Use "I" or "I am". "I (action or feeling)......" "I am ......" "Every day I....."
3. Write them in the present tense - as if you have already created a new habit or achieved a goal

4. Use positive language. Instead of "I don't eat junk food" make it "I enjoy eating food that is good for me"
5. Keep your statements short
6. Make your statements specific
7. Include action words and emotion or feeling words
8. Remember to keep them about you. What do you think? What do you feel? What do you say? What do you do? What have you achieved? If you want to see changes in the words and actions of the people around you then use your preferred reality scripts to change your thoughts, feelings, words and actions. When you change, other people will change how they respond to you.

Some reminders before we move on.

Our unconscious mind is working all the time to keep us within the bounds of what is familiar to us. It is working for you right now, so if you have never written a preferred reality script, your unconscious mind might be telling you that you don't need or want to do it. You might be having thoughts like "this is too hard" or "I just don't want to do it" or "this might have worked for Jennifer, but it won't work for me". If that is happening to you, this is the exact moment that you can choose to think differently and retrain your unconscious mind; after all, it is there to help you not limit you.

One of the ways your unconscious mind will work to resist the changes you want in your life is through inaction or procrastination. You will think you are going to get around to writing your preferred reality scripts, but you just never find the time to do it. Put some time aside in the next 24 to 48 hours and just start writing your preferred reality scripts. Give yourself permission to not get them exactly right straight away; you can go back and tweak them later.

Give yourself permission to invest some time and energy to create the future you want for yourself.

Think about it another way... you are already spending your time and energy, you are already thinking thoughts, you are already having feelings, you are already saying words, you are already engaged in activities. If you learn to consciously do these things in ways that benefit you, and if you persist with this new conscious thinking and actions, your unconscious mind will learn, and it will start to do them for you....winning.

You might already be a person who is familiar with and likes to use affirmations. If your affirmations complement your personal vision, your goals and your game plan, have "I am" or "I" in them, are in the present tense, use positive language, are short and specific, include action and emotion or feeling words and are about you, then just review them and keep practising them. If they don't, then write your preferred reality scripts, check that there is no conflict or contradiction between your affirmations and your preferred reality scripts and use both of them.

Actions to Create Your Preferred Reality

1. Over the coming days, take notice of what you think and say. Ask yourself if they are possible or impossible statements. Your impossible statements will include words like can't; words that limit your mind's ability to see the alternative options.

2. Use the eight tips I outlined earlier to help you write your Preferred Reality scripts.

3. If you have the **Good Life Game Plan** companion manual, review and do the activities in the **Preferred Reality Scripts** section.

In Part 10 you will learn how to turn your Preferred Reality Scripts into your **Life Songs**.

"Thoughts are like boomerangs, returning with precision to their source. Choose wisely which ones you throw."

Anonymous

PART 9

Lights... Camera... Action

Practice[4]
Noun
1. The actual application or use of an idea, belief, or method, as opposed to theories relating to it.
2. The customary, habitual, or expected procedure or way of doing something.
3. Repeated exercise in or performance of an activity or skill so as to acquire or maintain proficiency in it.

Now that we know how to create our **Good Life Game Plan** and **Preferred Reality Scripts** we can practice incorporating them into our daily life so that our unconscious mind starts to learn how to think and do the things that will create the life we want for ourselves.

Some people believe that they should just instantly know how to master a new skill or make an immediate change in their life. The reality is this belief sets them up for failure; it's an unrealistic expectation and does not give them the opportunity to make the changes they said they wanted in their life. This limiting belief can lead to disappointment, self-doubt, self-blame and negative self-talk. These are the perfect ingredients for giving up on your dreams.

The people who often succeed in life are the ones who believe things like;
It's ok to try things and fail
My mistakes are my best opportunity to learn
I will not let fear of judgement stop me from creating the life I want for myself.

Remember to regularly ask yourself, "What Am I Thinking?" and observe what you are saying.
If you are thinking or saying things like:
I can't do it
It's too hard
It's just the way I am
It's just not for me
I didn't really want it anyway
That did not work for me
It's someone or something else's fault
It's not fair
Other people will think I am silly if I...

STOP! You are now at a high level of risk of giving up on your dreams and your good life. Avoid making important decisions while you are in this limiting mindset. Take a minute, an hour or a day to allow your conscious mind to make the right decisions for you. Be kind to yourself and do some activities to help you get back into a solutions-focused mindset.

- Read your Letter to Me
- Have a look at your Dream Life Interview
- Check-in with your Personal Vision
- Do another Wheel of Life
- Meditate or listen to uplifting music
- Rest or sleep if that is what you need
- Do something mindful that you enjoy doing

In my childhood, learning did not always come easily to me. I suspect my teachers would have recognised me as a slow learner, and I often felt very inadequate and struggled in the school environment. For many years I have recognised the gifts contained within my childhood learning experiences. I accept that things did not come instantly and easily to me. In my teenage years, I acknowledged that I may need to ask more questions or that it might just take me longer to learn some things. In my adult life, I have consciously observed my strengths and weaknesses and made adjustments. I understand that my weaknesses do not make me less of a person. I developed a level of resilience and persistence in my attitude towards learning and making my good life.

Think about someone, or even yourself, mastering a particular skill set in sport, education, career, hobby or just in day to day life. We don't start as experts; we increase our ability by learning about it, thinking about it, making a plan and doing it. We might do it over and over and over again to become good at it and then we need to keep practising it. Becoming a master of our mind is the same. We need to learn about it, think about it, make a plan and do it. Then we need to practice it over and over and over again.

Some people will put time and effort into some areas of their life but not others. How many people do you know who put time and effort into their career and wealth creation but ignore their failing family relationships and/or their mental and physical health needs? Other people put time and effort into looking after their family and friends to only end up rundown and unwell themselves. Some people do things then feel guilty about it later because their actions harmed themselves or others.

We don't just magically know how to change our unconscious mind, but luckily there is an abundance of information and tools available to teach us how to do it. We will now look at some of the tools available. You might find the concept of doing it over and over and over again daunting, but it can be fun if you pick the mix of tools that are right for you.

Here is a list of potential tools. This is quite a big list and I recommend that you only pick one or two things initially. Once you get comfortable with incorporating those tools into your life you can come back and try other things from the list.

 **Thought Replacement**

As discussed above, you can regularly ask yourself, "What am I thinking? (W.A.I.T?)". With continued practice, you will start to catch yourself thinking thoughts that do not match your preferred reality. You might be lying awake running the same set of thoughts over and over in your head. If you know your preferred reality scripts, you can consciously replace those unwanted thoughts with your preferred reality scripts. It will take practice and persistence, but you can learn to replace your unwanted thoughts with your wanted thoughts.

LIGHTS... CAMERA... ACTION

Here are some methods you could use to actively incorporate your preferred reality scripts onto your daily life.

 **Visualisation/Mental Imagery**

Plan to sit quietly for 5 to 15 minutes. Preferably do this in a quiet place where you will not be disturbed, but there are also other options that I will discuss below.

Have your preferred reality scripts available to you - either written in a book, printed or on your device, or just know them. Pick one or more of your statements to visualise for that session.

If you can, close your eyes, relax your body and breath rhythmically and deeply 3 to 5 times.

Ask your mind to visualise a clear and detailed mental image of you being the person from your preferred reality script. Imagine you are that person and/or you have accomplished that thing. What would you see, hear, touch, smell and taste? What would you feel? Keep practising this visualisation once or twice a day.

If you're having difficulty finding the opportunity to sit quietly for 5 to 15 minutes, look for other opportunities. Next time you are waiting in the doctors' surgery, instead of reaching for your mobile phone to fill the time, visualise your preferred reality.

You can do this on a train, bus, plane, as a passenger in a car, anywhere you are sitting and waiting. You can do it if you are lying awake at night. You can do it in your lunch break. You can even learn to do it while you are walking. Keep an open mind so you can notice when your doors to opportunity are opened. Be ready to walk through that door, take action and create the life you want.

 **Vision Boards/ Dream Boards**

You can make vision and dream boards on your electronic devices, or you can get busy with paper, scissors and glue to create what your future looks like.

If you want to use your electronic devices, simply search for apps to use. My current favourite app is Canva and then there is Pinterest, Google Slides and many other apps available to help you create your vision board.

If you want to get hands-on arty, set yourself a date, gather up your equipment, create your space and get making. You can even do it with your family or friends, but don't let anyone delay or distract you from getting it done. You could make it an event or ceremony - light candles, listen to relaxing or uplifting music, have a cuppa or your favourite drink; just make sure you make it fun and get it done. The equipment you will need will include;
- corkboard/cardboard/whiteboard,
- paper, glue/pins/tape/magnets,
- coloured pencils/markers/paint,
- decorative paper,
- scissors,
- magazines,
- photos, printed images from online searches.

You might wonder what the difference is between a vision board and a dream board. This can be different things for different people.

LIGHTS... CAMERA... ACTION

For me: My vision board contains images and words about things that are achievable, with some planning and persistence, in the next one to six months. My dream board is exactly that; something that I dream about for my distant future.

My vision board has seven sections. I like to include things from many aspects of my life so that I know I am keeping some level of balance. I choose my seven sections from Health, Family, Relationships/Love, Social Activities, Financial/Wealth, Career/Livelihood/Education, Spirituality, Hobbies, Travel/Fulfillment.

I have three equal parts at the top and bottom of the page, which gives me six spaces to put images and words about six different aspects of my life. I devote the whole middle section to the aspect of my life that is currently most important for me to focus on and make changes to my current reality. In the image on the next page I have made Health and Wellbeing my highest priority, so I will include images and words relating to my health and wellbeing goals. It might be exercise, healthy food, drinking water, activities that I want to be able to do, clothes that I want to be able to wear etc.

Here is the layout of my vision board.

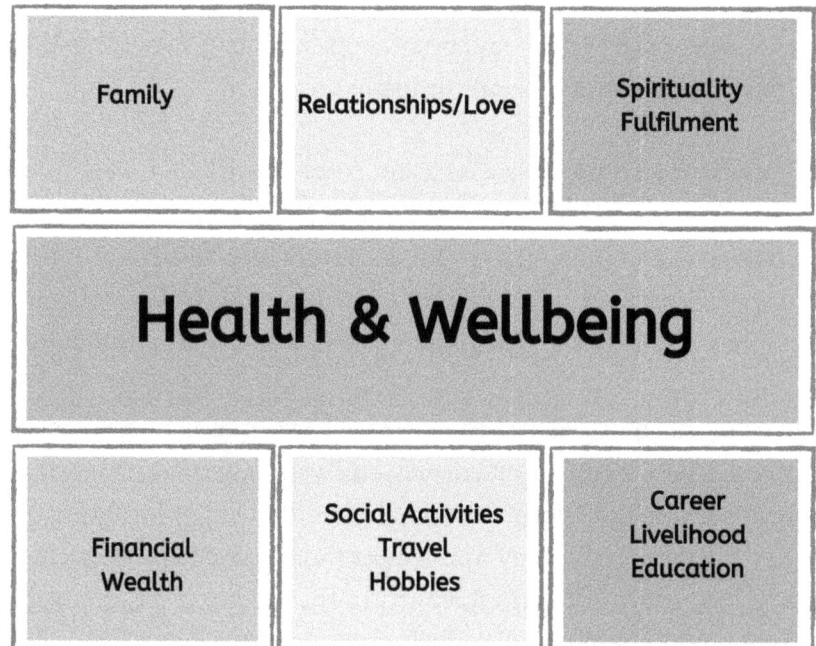

I want my vision board to show me my future reality as if it already existed.
I want my vision board to remind me of the words and actions I used to achieve that reality.
I want my vision board to inspire me.
I want to be able to look at my vision board and say to myself, yes, I want that in my life.

LIGHTS... CAMERA... ACTION

Here is an example of what a vision board could look like.

Finding the Images for Your Vision Board

Search the internet, magazines and your own photos for images that match your **Preferred Reality**. It is helpful to read through your **Good Life Game Plan,** your **Personal Vision** and your **Preferred Reality Scripts** to remind you what types of images you want. Save these images in a central location so they are easy to find when you are making your board.

Assembling Your Vision Board

Decide the layout of your board. What seven aspects will you include? What is your highest priority goal? Start putting your image/s and words in each section. Take the time to think about each image you use. If an image makes you feel that you are lacking something, don't use that image. Notice what you are thinking and feeling when you are looking at your images. If you don't believe that it is possible, then it is not possible. Thank yourself for noticing this limiting belief and write some more scripts to help you expand your mind to these new possibilities.

You can add things to your boards like drawings or symbols that have meaning to you.

Once you have finished your board, put it up somewhere so you can see it often. You don't have to put it up on public display, but you can if you want to. You just need to put it somewhere that you will see it. You could put it on the wall in your bedroom or behind the door, in your cupboard, in the bathroom, or even make it your phone's lock screen or computer screen saver. Just put it somewhere that you will look at it every day.

Now here is the important next step - look at it every day, think about what those images and words mean to you and how they make you feel, then take action to achieve those things on your board.

 **Phone and Computer Screensavers**

I mentioned above that you could put your vision board as your screensaver. I also often turn my personal statements into text images so that I can use them as screensavers on my mobile devices and computer. You can make your image with just text, or you can add a meaningful picture to the text. You can use any software that will convert your image to a .jpg or PNG. You need to consider the size and shape of the image to match the device you want to put on. I often use Canva, and there are many other free apps that can support this. Once I have my preferred reality script as my screensaver, I then have the opportunity to take a moment to read them before I unlock my device.

Word Maps

I learnt to create my word maps by reading, The Kindness Method: Changing Habits for Good by Shahroo Izadi. In this book, Shahroo teaches you how to be kind to yourself and develop a series of word maps to help you change your unwanted habits. This has assisted me to observe myself with kindness and curiosity and helped me better understand the false beliefs I held about myself and my life.

Passwords

We can often get frustrated with all the passwords we need to use daily, so many years ago I decided to use my passwords to my advantage. Each year I had a theme of something I wanted to change in my life, and I set my daily passwords to match that theme. Entering passwords no longer felt like a burden because I knew they were giving me daily opportunities to teach my unconscious mind about the life that I wanted for myself.

If I was thinking about my health life scripts, I could set a password like Good4mybody or Ilike2moveit. Remember to consider the security level when you are setting your preferred reality passwords.

Sticky Notes

It is very quick and easy to write your scripts or personal vision statement on sticky notes and put them anywhere you will get to read them.

Meditation

You can treat your meditations much like the visioning activity, or you can simply read your preferred reality scripts so they are fresh in your mind when you do your favourite meditation.

There are many free or paid apps, websites, videos, books and support groups that teach you different meditation techniques. Keep looking until you find some that work for you.

Listening to Music

There has been much discussion and research on how music affects the human brain and mood. Some studies suggest that listening to particular types of music while learning may improve the brain's ability to retain information. Baroque Largo Classical music is often suggested as good music for learning. A quick online search for classical Baroque Largo music will help you find some pieces that make you feel good. Sit and listen to the music while you visualise your preferred reality.

Practising Gratitude

There is an abundance of information available about how to practise gratitude. Think about how you can use gratitude to create your preferred reality from the things you already have in your life.

Law of Attraction

Research the Law of Attraction and consider how you can use this law to create your preferred reality.

Checklist

I love to tick things off my daily checklist. Those ticks are like little positive messages of achievement from me to me. That sense of achievement reminds me that I can do things and motivates me to keep going and tick more items off my daily checklist. If you are like me, you can use your preferred reality scripts to decide some of the things you want to put on your checklist for the day. They don't have to be big things, but every little tick is one step closer to your preferred reality.

Keeping a Diary

You might like to keep a diary about your preferred reality. You could write your statements in the front and then write about what you are thinking, feeling, saying and doing each day in relation to each statement. You might prefer to make it a visual, video or audio diary.

Goal Setting and Reminder Apps

There is plenty of information and apps available to support you with goal setting. I do get busy in my day, so I use a reminder app to remind me to do little things that match the person I want to be. It could be as simple as call Mum tonight, go for a walk or spend 30 minutes in the garden. I also use this app to help me keep my life organised and remind me of those little tasks I need to get done - pay that bill, book that flight, attend that meeting.

Poems/Prose

You could rewrite your preferred reality scripts into poems or prose. They will be easier to remember and more enjoyable for you to say them to yourself regularly.

Record Yourself Speaking Your Scripts

Pick your favourite instrumental music, record yourself speaking your preferred reality scripts and then mix it over the top of your instrumental music. If you know how to record and mix the music you can use your favourite software to do it yourself. If not, you can use apps like ThinkUp.

 ## Creating and Singing Your Life Songs

I like to sing my preferred reality. Singing makes me feel good, and I find it easier to remember my preferred reality scripts when I have turned them into songs.

I generally don't record my **Life Songs** because I want to consciously engage in singing my preferred reality. I also like to have the flexibility to change my songs whenever I want to. I might decide that a particular word or statement is a more suitable representation of my preferred reality. Nowadays, I often catch myself unconsciously singing my **Life Songs** and I smile because I know my unconscious mind will be working on creating it for me.

Onwards and Upwards

1. Pick one or two tools discussed in this section to incorporate your Preferred Reality scripts into your life. Use your preferred reality scripts daily to support you to stay with these new actions.

2. Look at your **Personal Vision** and **Good Life Game Plans** often and do the actions.

3. Be kind to yourself and keep practising, accept that you are learning and with persistence, you will make the changes you want in your life.

"Music
The magical,
Life-changing gift.
It is the shared love songs.
It is the celebrations in life.
It is the dancing in my kitchen.
It is the connection with others.
It is the rhythm in my heart, my hands, my body.
It is the loyal companion when all others are gone.
It is the hopes, the triumphs and the commiserations.
It is the power to instantly change how I feel and transform my mind."

Jennifer Emmett

PART 10

Cue the Music

Music[4]

Noun

1. Vocal or instrumental sounds (or both) combined in such a way as to produce beauty or form, harmony and expression of emotion.

Can you imagine a life without music? No music would mean:

No happy birthday song
No wedding songs
No funeral songs
No love songs
No protest songs

No uplifting songs
No hymns
No meditation music
No bands
No music performers
No dancing of any type
No dance clubs
No nightclubs
No concerts
No music at sporting events
No music in movies, theatre or plays.

We hear music because the soundwaves enter our ear and our cochlea turns this mechanical soundwave energy into electrical impulses in our mind. These electrical impulses move through our brain stem and activate the limbic system and stimulate motor responses and emotions. The music also moves to the conscious part of the brain and has the ability to tap both sides of the brain and build neural connections between the left & right brain[6].

We literally feel the music; we feel emotions generated by the rhythm, the melody, the instruments, and the singing. We also feel the pulse of the sound waves as they interact with our bodies. When we are feeling music, we can be in the moment, and music makes a difference in how we think, feel and act!

If you do a search on the internet you will find millions of sites discussing the beneficial effects of music on the brain. Listening to music is often prescribed as one of the ways to support our health and wellbeing, including:

- Improve mood and reduce depression[7]
- Maximise learning and improve memory[8]
- Reduce stress and anxiety[8]
- Improve performance[8]
- Help ease pain[7]
- Help us relax and go to sleep[8]

We are encouraged to use music to support our children with brain growth, language skills, maths skills, memory, attention and concentration, increased coordination, achievement and discipline, social skills, joy and for life[9].

I briefly discussed in Part 1 how music assisted me through a period of depression. Since then, music has been a very important part of my life. I have spent many joyous hours experimenting with all sorts of instruments, writing and singing. I never became a particularly talented performer but that was not the point of why I was doing it. I was playing with musical instruments and singing because I liked the way it made me feel. I liked that it gave me a new way of connecting with myself and others. After a few years I found a particular affinity with the Djembe Drum and traditional rhythms. I spent years learning how to get rhythm in my body, just because I liked the way it made me feel. Through this learning I gained skills and knowledge that I was able to share with others and I went on to teach and share Djembe Drumming with hundreds of people. I joined a band and met my wife, and we continued to play music together for years. So much friendship and joy has come through the sharing of music and it is often the thing I turn to when I am feeling overwhelmed or distressed about events in my life.

Back in 2014, when I started providing mindset coaching to the people around me, I understood that music could have a powerful effect on our thoughts and feelings.

I recorded myself speaking my own preferred reality scripts and mixed them to instrumental music tracks. This meant that I could go for my morning walk or do other tasks and listen to my own voice speaking my own future life while also listening to music that I enjoyed.

After a time, I concluded that this process did not have the impact that I had hoped for and I wondered why. I eventually came to the conclusion that even though I was regularly hearing the words, my mind was not actively engaging in them. I could easily be distracted by other thoughts. Over time I started to turn my preferred reality scripts into my own songs. These were not songs to record and just listen to, these were songs that I sang to myself. By singing them, I was actually saying the words and my mind was learning and changing.

This worked for me, so I started turning more of my personal statements into songs.

I created My Career & Financial song, My Health song, My Love Song and My Abundance Song.

In this section, I am sharing a method you can use to create your own Life Songs.

Keep It Simple

When I first started thinking about turning my preferred reality scripts into songs, I got all over-complicated about it. I was thinking I was going to have to write and record original music and then record myself singing the songs and mix it with the music. I started to worry about how I was going to make it sound good enough in the recording. I went through this whole process of thinking I would need to pay a professional singer to sing my songs for me and blah blah blah - way over-complicated. I then came to the conclusion that I was creating a whole lot of unnecessary work to achieve my desired outcome.

All I really wanted was to be easily able to recall my preferred reality scripts and remind myself of them daily by singing them. I also wanted to put them to music that made me feel good and excited about my preferred reality. I realised that I did not need original music, or to record anything, or to even make it sound good to anyone else.

These songs are written by me, for me, about my life. I sing them to me; I don't need anybody's approval to sing them and I don't need to worry if anyone else will like them. They are my songs - if I like them, they are the right songs for me.

The beauty of this is that I can create any song I want, and even change the words when I want to. My songs often morph as the possibilities expand in my own mind.

It can be a 10-second song or a 5 minute song; you just need to know all the words.

There are thousands of highly talented artists who have already recorded hundreds of thousands of songs that I could choose from. I went to my favourites playlists and started to pick out songs that I loved. I was not that concerned with the current words of the song as I knew I would change most of the words.

I thought about the tempo and how that music makes me feel.

For example, I picked a very upbeat song for my health song because I wanted it to help me feel exhilarated and get me up and moving. I often dance when I am singing my health song.

I also may not use the full song; I might only need a part of the song to write my message to myself. Once I chose the song, I noted how many syllables in each of the lines I wanted to use. I then experimented with how I could rewrite a line or lines of my preferred reality script to match the number of syllables, or thereabouts.

I wrote and tested singing my words to the music. I worked on it over a few days until I got the meaning of my preferred reality scripts to fit the song. It did not always sound that great initially, but after I had practised it for a few days, it started to become smoother and I would think of other ways to tweak it.

Here is a simple example of changing a well-known song into a basic wealth song.

Song: Happy Birthday.
Preferred Reality Scripts: Money comes to me easily and effortlessly.
Money creates a positive impact on my life.

CUE THE MUSIC

Original Lyrics	Syllables	New Lyrics
Happy Birthday to you	6	Money comes to me
Happy Birthday to you	6	Positive in my life
Happy Birthday dear (your name)	7 to 10ish	Easily and happily
Happy Birthday to you	6	Lots of money comes to me

In the above example, I changed the word "effortlessly" to "happily" because I wanted to make it easier to sing. I also added extra syllables to the last line because it sounded ok to me to fit those syllables.

Your main goal is to create a song that:
- You can remember
- Is easy and fun for you to sing
- Gives you the message that will reprogram your autopilot.

Let's have a go at another version.

Original Lyrics	Syllables	New Lyrics
Happy Birthday to you	6	Abundant money
Happy Birthday to you	6	Rains down upon me
Happy Birthday dear (your name)	7 to 11	I use it for higher good
Happy Birthday to you	6	And more money comes to me

Original Lyrics	Syllables	New Lyrics
Happy Birthday to you	6	Money is my friend
Happy Birthday to you	6	With wisdom I spend
Happy Birthday dear (your name)	7 to 11	Money is good for you and me
Happy Birthday to you	6	And I am very wealthy

How would you like to word it?

Original Lyrics	Syllables	New Lyrics
Happy Birthday to you	6	
Happy Birthday to you	6	
Happy Birthday dear (your name)	7 to 11	
Happy Birthday to you	6	

You could make your wealth song very short, or you could extend it.

In the example below, I have used the above examples to make it a three-part song.

My Wealth Song
Money comes to me
Positive in my life
Easily and happily
Lots of money comes to me

CUE THE MUSIC

Abundant money
Rains down upon me
I use it for higher good
And more money comes to me

Money is my friend
With wisdom I spend
Money is good for you and me
And I am very wealthy

Now that I have written my Wealth Song lyrics, I can just sing it to the Happy Birthday tune, or I might decide to try it out to other tunes.

My main goal is to know the words, say them often and have feelings about them that support me to stick to my Game Plan. I am using my **Life Songs** to reprogram my autopilot to support me in living my preferred reality.

In the above examples I have used a very simple, universally-known song to explain my process. You can pick the songs that you love and your own words to make your **Life Songs**.

Remember you don't have to use the full song and you are not making it for performance or recording. You are making it for you; you are creating a tool to support you to create the life that you want.

So often when I talk to people about music and singing they are quick to tell me that they can't sing and have no musical ability. They don't even let themselves sing to themselves when they are alone.

Have you ever been told by a parent, sibling, kids, partner, teacher or anyone else that you can't sing? If you asked 100,000 people this question, the majority would say yes.

The sad thing is that many of these people then believed that they could not sing and so stopped singing. The truth is if you have a voice you can sing. Even if you don't have a voice, you can sing in your mind.

It is a popular belief in our society that we should only sing if we have the talent to do so. Imagine if we applied this same belief to other activities in our life.

We would say things like:

"I used to love tennis, but I can't play social tennis or join the tennis club because I tried it when I was younger, and I did not make it into the state/national team, so I was just not good enough to play tennis."

"In my earlier years when I tried dancing, I never won a dance competition and did not get selected for the blah blah dance troupe. That means I can never dance in public or when I am alone."

"I don't cook because my food doesn't taste as nice as a chef's."

Those statements sound ridiculous because they are ridiculous, and so is the belief that you can't sing. We humans started singing because it makes us feel good, it connects us, and it is good for our mind and body.

It just happens that some people are elite singers and performers, and they make it to the top of their field. That does not mean that the rest of us should stop doing it.

If you have stopped singing due to this false belief, get your voice back and sing; it is uplifting and good for you.

It can be easy to trick yourself into thinking that you don't have enough time to write and sing your own songs. That is your unconscious mind keeping you on track with the things it currently knows and believes about who you are. This is the moment where you can say, I can do this, and I do have the time to take this action to change my mind and change my life.

While you are doing other things, you can be recalling or noticing songs that you like.

You can experiment with different line structures and words to add your preferred reality scripts to those songs.

You might question how a person who is deaf or hearing impaired can gain benefit from music. Deaf people can enjoy music in ways that differ from how hearing people enjoy music, and they can derive pleasure out of it. First of all, deafness does not necessarily mean that someone does not hear anything at all – there are varying levels of deafness. Secondly, deaf people can feel the vibrations produced by the music being played and consume those vibrations through their body[10].

Actions to write your first **Life Song**

1. Find 5 to 10 songs that you really like and enjoy singing along to. You are looking for songs that create positive emotions and that you can comfortably sing (at least parts of the song).
2. Write the song title, how that song makes you feel, where can you easily find that song when you need it, and what you might like to use that song for, e.g. Career Song, Love Song, Friendship Song, Health Song, Travel Song, Abundance Song, Family Song, Wealth Song, Adventure Song etc..
3. Pick your Preferred Reality Scripts that you want to put to that song.

4. Write out the current song lyrics, allowing space to write your lyrics next to each line.
5. Pick which part of your Preferred Reality Script you are going to put in each line and rearrange or replace the words to fit the syllables or flow of each line.
6. Keep singing and rearranging it until you're happy with it.

If you have the **Good Life Game Plan** companion manual, you can utilise the **My Life Song** section to assist you with this process.

Afterword

The teenage version of me concluded that I was a complete dreamer. Many days I would wake up with my mind full of exciting things I wanted to do only to find that at the end of the day I had not completed any of them. I was easily side-tracked and lived in a kind of a dream world, but it was not until I was in my 30's that I came to understand more fully what was actually going on.

I became aware that I regularly created different life stories in my own mind. These stories often had themes of escapism or arguments with past and present people in my life. They were not true; they were acts that played out in my mind and impacted my understanding of my reality. I often felt an overwhelming sense of depression, I had thoughts of suicide and I kept a very high level of emotional detachment from the people who offered me friendship.

I can remember the day that I recognised it was happening - I was standing at the kitchen sink and had washed, dried and put the dishes away, and then I was polishing the sink. All that time I was playing out an argument with some friends in my mind. At some point, as I was playing out what they had said or done, I said to myself, "Wait that's not true! That's not even possible! What am I thinking? Why am I thinking about this?".

Have you ever seen the movie "The Secret Life of Walter Mitty"? Walter Mitty spent much of his life living in an alternative reality, and when I saw that movie I realised that there must be other people who had that same experience as me.

Over the coming weeks and months, I traced back through the years and found the signs that I had been playing out these unreal stories in my mind for many years. I was discovering within myself something that I later came to understand happens to all humans in one form or another. In his talk "Your brain hallucinates your conscious reality" British professor of Cognitive and Computational Neuroscience, Anil Seth, explains how our brain uses the information that is available to it, to make its best prediction of our current reality and how we accept that prediction as the truth.

I had also developed some knowledge of the law of attraction; I knew I did not want to be sending negative thoughts out because I understood that these negative thoughts would attract negative actions in my life.

In recognising my thought patterns, I had given myself an important opportunity to make a change in my life. I set myself on a path of being more conscious of what I was thinking, and when I caught myself entering into delusional thought patterns, I would consciously

AFTERWORD

make an effort to stop those thoughts. It did not come easily, and I regularly slipped back into my old thinking habits. Over time I learnt that it was helpful to have another set of thoughts ready to replace my unwanted negative thoughts. I then understood the power of preparing my own **Preferred Reality Scripts** and practising them often so I could easily recall them when I really needed them. Eventually, I learned that turning them into my **Life Songs** was the best way for me to be thinking about the things that are good to me.

I now regularly catch myself singing my own songs in my mind. I am delighted when this happens because I know that these songs are full of statements that are good for me. It has been years since I had thoughts of suicide, and I continue to regularly ask myself, **"What Am I Thinking?** Do these thoughts help me to live my good life?".

In this book, I have written about conscious thinking, conscious words and conscious actions to help us change our unconscious thinking, unconscious words and unconscious actions. I believe it has been a valuable investment of my time and money to learn and develop these practices in my life. I have often pushed myself beyond my comfort zone to create my preferred reality.

I equally value when I have allowed myself the time and space to just be me. There have been times when my mental energy was very low, so I stopped pushing myself. I gave myself permission to rest. I gave myself permission to do whatever I felt like doing at that very moment in time. Some of my greatest creations, experiences and knowings came to me in those times of just being.

I continue on my pursuit of knowing and doing, and I continue to look for ways to balance this with just being me.

BEYOND POSSIBLE

I have learnt that there are some things I innately know - it's like a sense of knowing that comes from my very being - there are some things I can learn to know, and there are some things I will never know, and I am ok with that.

My wish for you is a good life and that you go beyond your current possible.

Namaste,
Jennifer

Appendices

My Good Life/Dream Year

Imagine that starting today, you are living your good life! Your fulfilling life! I am not talking about the life you think others expect you to want or that you think you should want. I am talking about the life that you truly want for yourself! Imagine that you are living your dream year. What is your dream year like? What are you like? What things do you do? How do you behave? What are the people around you like? What sorts of things do you have?

Take a couple of minutes to jot down the things that would make life good for you. You don't need to spend much time on this; there are more activities in this book to help you think more about this.

Letter To Me

Write a letter to yourself. It is like a map that you can look at if you start to feel lost and will help guide you as you move to your good life. Your letter can look something like this:

Dear (your name),

It's (today's date), you are (where you are right now and briefly describe what is happening in your life right now). You have decided to make a change/s because……..You're tired of……..You have been promising yourself for years that you would…….You finally need to……

It's time you stopped….. It's time you started…. This is really important because…. It's time to be honest with yourself and admit that…..

Your resistance to change has meant that…..

If over the coming weeks you start thinking that this is not important, remember that….. If you start finding it harder than expected remember to push through because….. You need to take this seriously because…..You had hoped by now that….. If you don't find your own way to do this now, you will end up having to…. You want to feel like you are….

My Dream Life Interview

In this activity, you play the roles of both the interviewer and the interviewee. You are encouraged to treat it like a game and have fun with both roles. Make sure you follow the game rules and complete the interview, but make sure you don't take yourself too seriously during the interview process. If you like, you can create a character for your interviewer - they might have an accent, be from a different time or be your favourite character in a movie or book that you love. They might be someone you know and admire. In the role of interviewee, be authentically yourself and as honest as you can.

Allow 30 to 60 minutes and ensure the interview is conducted in a quiet/private space.

The Interviewer Rules
Yourself or role-playing as a character
- Remove external distractions (your very important interviewee deserves your full and undivided attention for the full interview). Turn off phones, iPads, TV.
- Ask the questions listed below and give the interviewee plenty of time to answer.
- Write the answers to the questions in your notebook.
- Show patience, care, respect, and genuine interest in the interviewee.
- Be kind, gentle and encouraging to your interviewee.
- Never share the interviewee's dreams with someone else, without their permission.
- Your role in this interview is to support the interviewee to answer all the questions and feel comfortable about their answers.
- If you have questions that are not listed below, ask them (make sure they are non-judgemental).
- Ask the interviewee if they have any other dreams to share.
- Look up Edward de Bono - Six Thinking Hats - As the interviewer, you are wearing the Yellow Hat, which symbolises brightness and optimism.

- Ensure you keep the yellow hat on and do not switch to the black hat, which is the Logical Negative - Careful and cautious, the judgment hat.

The Interviewee Rules
- Be authentically yourself.
- The interviewer will remove all external distractions (you are very important to the interviewer and they deserve your full and undivided attention for the full interview). Turn off phones, iPads, TV.
- Answer all the questions. The interviewer will give you the time you need to answer each question.
- The interviewer will write down your answers but don't worry, you can change your answers.
- Allow your dreams to flow openly; say whatever you feel like saying, do not limit your answers. There is NO wrong answer.
- The interviewer will never share your answers with anyone else unless you give them permission to do so.
- If you have dreams to share that the interviewer did not ask you about, share them.
- Look up Edward de Bono - Six Thinking Hats. As the interviewee, you can wear the Green hat which focuses on creativity: the possibilities, alternatives and new ideas, Red hat which signifies feelings, hunches and intuition and Yellow hat which symbolises brightness and optimism.
- Ensure you do not switch to the black hat at any time through this dream interview process. The black hat is the Logical Negative - Careful and cautious, the judgment hat.
- You will have the opportunity to put the Black Hat on in your Dream Filter.

APPENDICES

Interview Questions
What inspires you?
What are your passions?
How can you make the world better?
What did you enjoy doing as a child?
What does success look like to you?
What does your ideal day look and feel like?
Is there anything you would like to learn?
What would be your ideal social life?
What would help you feel financially secure?
What would be your ultimate health and wellbeing status?
What are your relationship dreams (partner/family/friends)?
What is your current age and how long do you plan to live for?
If you only had six months to live...what would you want to do in those six months?
Interviewer impromptu questions (optional)

My Life Planning App Questions
In Part 5, I discussed My Life Planning App. Here are the current questions on my app with a focus on my health goal.

Section 1.
This is a note to me. It might be a list of my current goals, my personal vision statement or anything else I want to remind myself about, especially when my life starts to get out of balance.

Section 2.
Today's Date
- My level of exercise today (1 is Low - 10 is I rocked it).
- My food today (1 = I Stuffed myself with sugar and carbs - 10 = I ate a good amount of healthy food).

- Family Relationships (1 = Needs significant change - 10 = Just the way I like it)
- Financial (1 = Needs significant change - 10 = Just the way I like it)
- Mental and Spiritual (1 = Needs significant change - 10 = Just the way I like it)
- Physical Health (1 = Needs significant change - 10 = Just the way I like it)
- Social (1 = Needs significant change - 10 = Just the way I like it)
- Career (1 = Needs significant change - 10 = Just the way I like it)
- Today's life fulfilment rating (1 = Needs significant change - 10 = Just the way I like it)
- What would I like to change?
- What have I been dreaming about doing or being?
- Any actions/comments
- Three things I am grateful for today

The best thing about creating your own questionnaire is that you can create the questions to exactly match your current goals.

Current Reality to Preferred Reality

Current Reality
Use a sentence or short paragraph to describe each of the following aspects of your life.
Health
Family
Relationships
Social Activities

Financial
Livelihood
Spiritual

Preferred Reality
Now describe how you would prefer things to be.
Health
Family
Relationships
Social Activities
Financial
Livelihood
Spiritual

How I Spend my Time

Describe what you do on an average day. Who do you spend your time with? What activities do you do? What sort of things do you think about? Are you involved in recreational, learning, exercise, spiritual or social activities? Think about your typical morning, afternoon, evening and night. Write a short paragraph or dot points about each of these four parts of your typical day.

Think about your life outside of work. Write a short paragraph or dot points to describe what you do on an average week, month and year.

My Health

Think about your mental and physical health. How would you describe your current health? Do you currently have habits that do not support your good health? What activities do you do to support your good health? Is there anything going on that you could seek support for? Are you avoiding getting support for your health needs? If yes, do you know why you would be avoiding getting support with your health needs? What actions can you take and what new habits can you create to support your mental and physical health?

Learn and Grow

What sort of things do you do to learn and grow? What are the types of things that you read about? How do you expose yourself to new ideas and new ways of thinking?

Finances

What sorts of things do you do to manage your finances?

About the Author

Jennifer Emmett was born in Gippsland, Victoria. Her family moved to Queensland when she was still a toddler. She spent her childhood in regional Queensland towns, including Beerburrum, Longreach, Kilcoy and Caboolture. In her late teenage years, Jennifer moved to Brisbane and after seven years in the city, she followed her yearning to head north. She lived in Townsville until 1994 before discovering her love of the Mackay region, where she continues to live to this day with her wife, Karen and their dogs Jed and Abby. As a child, Jennifer struggled in the education system. She left school at 16 years of age to discover her own ways of learning. Her innate curiosity about business, leadership, the human mind and how to live a good life has resulted in a life of discovery and achievement. Jennifer commenced working in leadership roles when she was 18 years of age and later became a company CEO. After ten years in this role, Jennifer decided to establish her own business, The Village Leaders.

Jennifer has a Diploma in Business and an Advanced Diploma in Community Sector Management. She values music and creativity in her life and has spent over 20 years facilitating Djembe Drumming workshops and community drum circles.

Through The Village Leaders, Jennifer combines her vast management and leadership experience with her musical and creative nous to provide Team and Personal Development, Leadership Coaching, Project Management and Community Engagement services to publicly and privately funded organisations and individuals.

Jennifer's contact details
Web: www.jenniferemmett.com.au
Web: www.thevillageleaders.com.au
Email: jennifer@jenniferemmett.com.au

More Testimonials

For over 50 years I have been an avid listener and reader of self-help manuals inspired by ancient wisdom, gurus and contemporary authors but never have I read the "how" to create change and balance to the depth of understanding in just one book. Authored by a special human being whom my husband and I are honoured to call friend, we celebrate and congratulate Jennifer's raw and honest account of her life journey which has shaped who she is today. A friend who willingly shares life events with us and the many who will benefit from reading "Beyond Possible." Jennifer has been responsible for inspiring us to reignite our passion in playing African Djembe. A teacher of African Drumming, Jennifer's style of teaching encourages us to dig deep from a place of joy, fun and much laughter without judgement. It's the nature of who she is. Jennifer is responsible for bringing together a core family of drummers. We are a multi-disciplined and multi-faceted multi-cultural bunch guided by Jennifer's ability to recognise the sameness in all of us – the sharing of playing djembe without judgement, with encouragement and with vision. Beyond Possible is supported by a companion "Game Plan" book to be released which demonstrates the essence of our teacher Jennifer throughout. We feel sure both books will become part of your reading and inspired life change. Congratulations Jennifer and thank you for inspiring us to look beyond the possible.

Rikki Kemp, Bachelor of Social Work (BSW) and
Philip Kemp, Traditional Custodian/Cultural Trainer

I have often tried to fix things around the house without much success. Imagine how much easier it would be with the right tools and suggestions on how I might be able to fix it. Through this book, Jennifer explores a range of life tools and how she has used them. As a community leader, Jennifer uses this book to share ideas that can inspire you to make your imagined good life a reality. Through this book, she is able to share her ideas as a mentor and friend.

Brentyn Parkin, Executive Director

Free Good Life Tools

You can download your Free Good Life Tools including **The Wheel of Life**, the **ABCDE for My Feelings and Actions** and the **My Life Planning App** from The Village Leaders website. www.thevillageleaders.com.au

If you would like to do more learning and activities to create the life you desire, Jennifer has designed the following bundles for you.

The Good Life Bundles

What You Get	Good Life Game Plan	Good Life Full Membership
Good Life Game Plan Workbook	✓	✓
My Good Life Online Course	✓	✓
Beyond Possible Ebook	✓	✓
My Good Life Secret Facebook Group Lifetime Membership	✗	Lifetime Membership
Weekly Q&A Session	✗	Lifetime Membership
My Good Life Masterminds	1 Free	Unlimited
Assistance to Complete Your Good Life Songs	✗	2 Songs
Onboard One on One Call	✗	30 to 45 minute call
Upgrade to Full Membership At Anytime	✓	

The Good Life Gift Pack

Give the gift of a Good Life for only $49.00

We will gift wrap and send the Beyond Possible book directly to you or a friend.
Plus
Both you and your friend will receive a 20% discount coupon on the Good Life Game Plan.

That's over $240.00 value.

Imagine sharing a life-changing adventure with someone important to you!

Source:

[1] https://en.wikipedia.org/wiki/Johari_window
[2] https://en.wikipedia.org/wiki/There_are_known_knowns
[3] https://en.wikipedia.org/wiki/Computer
[4] https://www.lexico.com/
[5] https://en.wikipedia.org/wiki/Brain_activity_and_meditation
[6] http://www.melodiousmerchant.com/percussionist-profundus/musicians-index-of-blogs-by-jack-bell/life-without-music/
[7] https://www.health.harvard.edu/staying-healthy/music-and-health
[8] https://www.fnu.edu/benefits-studying-music/
[9] https://www.learningpotential.gov.au/musical-benefits
[10] https://assistivetechnologyblog.com/2016/06/can-deaf-people-hear-music-answer-yes.html

Lightning Source UK Ltd.
Milton Keynes UK
UKHW010700281220
375839UK00001B/106